CLOUDS
AND GLORY

YEAR A

PRAYERS FOR THE CHURCH YEAR

CLOUDS AND GLORY

DAVID ADAM

MOREHOUSE PUBLISHING
Harrisburg, Pennsylvania

First published in Great Britain in 2000 by
The Society for Promoting Christian Knowledge (SPCK)

Morehouse Publishing
P.O. Box 1321
Harrisburg, PA 17105

Cataloging-in Publication Data is available from the Library of Congress.
ISBN 0-8192-1887-1

Cover design by Trude Brummer.

Printed in Great Britain
01 02 03 04 05   10 9 8 7 6 5 4 3 2 1

Contents

Introduction   1

ADVENT   5

CHRISTMAS   15

EPIPHANY   22

ORDINARY TIME   34

LENT   45

EASTER   58
  Ascension   72
  Pentecost   77

ORDINARY TIME   80
  Bible Sunday   136
  Dedication Festival   138
  All Saints' Day   140

SUNDAYS BEFORE ADVENT   143
  Christ the King   150

Introduction

In the parish church on Holy Island the east window depicts the Ascension. Almost at the apex of this window is a cloud and above that the sun. Because the disciples are below the cloud I often wonder if they are aware of the glory beyond. I ask you, 'Are you aware of the glory that pervades all things?'

It was a Jew, but I know it could only be a person of prayer, who wrote the following on the wall of a prison cell in Cologne as they awaited persecution or death:

I believe in the sun even when it is not shining.
I believe in love even when I cannot feel it.
I believe in God even when he is silent.

So I seek to believe in the presence and love of God even though a cloud hides him from my sight. Time and time again I turn to the prayer from the Hebrides that says, 'Though the dawn breaks cheerless on this isle today, my spirit walks in a path of light.' I seek to know that both are real, the cloud and the glory: cloud, mist, misfortune, illness and darkness are all ever so real and there is no escaping them in this world; but there in the darkness is the Divine Presence. Even in our doubt he never leaves or forsakes us.

When I lived on the North Yorkshire Moors, I discovered what to do when the low cloud descended and made everything dull and grey – move from where you are! No, I do not recommend running away, only a change of perspective. I used to take the car up onto a moorland ridge road, no distance from

1

home, for the tops of the moors were sticking out of the cloud and in the sunshine. If the days had been long and dreary, this often really felt like breaking through into glory. Up above the cloud was a different world, yet part of the same one in reality. Here was brightness and light; even the clouds that filled the dales looked brighter and lighter from this side. I tried to have a spell up there in the brightness before returning to the greyness of the dale for I knew that such a walk would help me through the gloom of the day ahead.

Some people try to do the same with what they call 'positive thinking'. I am sure many benefit from this, and positive thinking is a help, but sometimes it is just positively stupid because it does not face the facts of what is really happening. Positive thinking is often a pretend world and not truly dealing with what is around us. If life is to be balanced, we need to face the whole of reality; and that involves cloud as well as glory.

Intercession is not positive thinking, it is facing the real situation in the presence and power of God. It is the attempt to hold the deepest of realities together, to pierce the obvious clouds to see the hidden presence; to get a glimpse of the glory, that we might have strength to walk in the darkness. As I would often take people with me out of the low cloud and into the sunshine, I seek to do the same in intercession: I seek to pierce the clouds and behold the glory. I approach God carrying people in my heart and prayers; I seek to discover that they are already in the heart of God and on their way to glory. I seek to hold on to the two realities; amidst the troubles and darkness of this world, we are all encircled and enclosed in the light, love and presence of our God. In doing this I move out of the cloud and towards the glory. Learn to walk in the light, to lead others and uplift others into that light, that you may know the power and the glory of our God.

I believe that one of the best preparations for Sunday worship is to use the readings for the coming Sunday throughout the week as an inspiration for prayer and intercession. As a young man, I used to use the same Collect, Epistle and Gospel every day from the Sunday through to the Saturday. By the Saturday I often knew the readings reasonably well and began to grasp their content – but there was a new set on the Sunday. I feel now that I had somehow got this the wrong way around: if we used the same readings from Monday to Sunday, when we came together on the Sunday how greatly our worship would be enriched. A wonderful preparation for Sunday is to pray every day of the week before the Sunday. No wonder worship in church is impoverished if we are not praying daily. If possible, use the readings set for the Sunday ahead to inspire and direct your prayers, then when we come together in worship it will be full of depth and meaning.

This book of intercessions is to help you along that path and, I hope, give you a glimpse beyond the clouds. It is written so that you can use it at home and so enrich your own prayers. Each week I would hope that you extend the ideas for prayer I have offered. As this book is laid out, it corresponds to the Common Worship Lectionary as adopted by the Church of England, the Scottish Episcopal Church, the Church in Wales and other churches within the Anglican Communion. This is very close to the Common Lectionary of the Roman Catholic Church and is used by other denominations. The Lectionary is designed as a three-year cycle and this book is for use with the first year of that cycle, designated as 'Year A'. For every week I have provided an extra prayer to centre us down and direct our thoughts, a list of intercessions, an offering of the peace and a blessing. As each week stands, it could be used for a short service in the home, or with a group. The intercessions follow the pattern as in many books of prayer: we pray, in order, for the church, the world, our homes and loved ones, the sick and needy, and remember the saints and the departed. If we add the readings from the Lectionary to the prayers in this book and give some time to quiet and meditation, it will transform our worship at home and in our local church. Use this book as a vehicle to get yourself out of the clouds and the greyness to where you get a glimpse of glory.

Advent

The First Sunday of Advent

Isaiah 2. 1–5 : Ps. 122 : Romans 13. 11–14 : Matthew 24. 36–44

Lord, we watch, we wait,
we look, we long for you.
Dispel the clouds and darkness
and awaken us to your glory,
that we may walk in your light,
through Jesus Christ our Lord. **Amen.**

Lord, you are ever among us.
Open our eyes to your presence,
that your church may be true to its mission,
that each congregation may proclaim your goodness,
that all of us may show forth your glory.
Lord, come down,
come in, come among us.

To the nations that are looking for freedom,
to the peoples that are longing for liberty,
to the individuals striving for justice,
to all who are seeking to improve the world,
to all who are seeking to improve themselves,
Lord, come down,
come in, come among us.

To our homes as we prepare for your coming,
to our loved ones as they reveal to us your love,
to our work, that it may show forth your presence,
into our leisure and into our pleasures,
Lord, come down,
come in, come among us.

To all who long for release,
to all who cry in pain,
to the sick in body, in mind and in spirit,
to those who can no longer cope,
to all who are oppressed and in darkness,
to all who watch and wait and weep for you,
Lord, come down,
come in, come among us.

That we may know that life is eternal,
that loved ones departed are in your keeping,
that we may rejoice in hope,
that we may come to your glory,
Lord, come down,
come in, come among us.

THE PEACE

May you see the glory of God in every place, and in every face;
and the peace of the Lord be always with you
and also with you.

THE BLESSING

God, who ever comes to you, draw you to his love, draw you to
his light, draw you to himself; and the blessing of God
Almighty, the Father, the Son and the Holy Spirit, be among
you, and remain with you always. **Amen.**

The Second Sunday of Advent

Isaiah 11. 1–10 : Ps. 72. 1–7 [18–19] : Romans 15. 4–13 : Matthew 3. 1–12

In God's power, in his peace, in his presence,
   we place ourselves today.
Holy God, Holy and Strong One, Holy and Mighty One,
protect us by your power, provide us with your peace,
fill our lives with your presence,
and awaken us to your coming;
through Jesus Christ the King of Glory,
who is alive and reigns with you and the Holy Spirit,
now and for ever. **Amen.**

Lord of righteousness, you yearn for the salvation
   of your people.
Forgive your church as it wastes its gifts
   and misuses its resources.
Increase in us deeper relationships and greater sensitivity.
Give us a zeal for your gospel and to proclaim your love.
Let our lives be good examples to others.
We pray for the church to which we belong,
   that it may be open to you.
We pray for the work of the whole church,
   that it may proclaim you.
O Lord, raise up, we pray, your power
and come among us.

We pray for world rulers, statesmen and politicians
that they may discover the road that leads to peace,

that they may accept the peace you offer them,
that captives may be freed,
the oppressed find relief,
the weary find rest,
the hungry find sustenance and the homeless shelter.
We pray for all relief organizations
and for all who seek to bring in your kingdom.
O Lord, raise up, we pray, your power
and come among us.

That our hearts may be opened to your coming in others,
to see you in our loved ones,
to see you in our neighbours and in our friends;
that we may welcome you in the stranger and the needy;
that we may serve you in the service of others;
O Lord, raise up, we pray, your power
and come among us.

That the ill and the housebound may behold traces of your
   glory;
that the despairing and depressed may find new hope;
that the lonely and the neglected may know your love;
that those who walk in darkness may know your light;
that all in weakness may find strength in you;
O Lord, raise up, we pray, your power
and come among us.

That the departed may rejoice in eternal life;
that they may be numbered with your saints in glory,
O Lord, raise up, we pray, your power
and come among us.

The God of hope fill you with all joy and peace in believing, so that you may abound in hope; and the peace of the Lord be always with you
and also with you.

THE BLESSING

The Lord open your eyes to his coming,
open your ears to his voice,
open your hearts to his love;
and the blessing of God Almighty, the Father, the Son and the Holy Spirit, be among you, and remain with you always. **Amen.**

The Third Sunday of Advent

———

Isaiah 35. 1–10 : Ps. 146. 5–10 : *or Canticle*: Magnificat : James 5. 7–10 : Matthew 11. 2–11

Almighty God, who through the prophets promised that light would conquer the darkness, shine in our hearts and in our minds, and so use us that we may lead others to your splendour and the greatness of your power which is revealed in your Son Jesus Christ, who lives with you and the Holy Spirit, One God, now and for ever. **Amen.**

Come, Lord God,
give strength to the hands that are tired
and to the knees that tremble with weakness.

You are the God who cares for all who are down,
you come down to where we are to uplift us.
You are the God who gives us hope.
You come to rescue us.
Come, Lord our Saviour.

Lord, may your church travel the road of holiness,
may we grow in faith, grow in love, and grow in number.
We pray for the church to which we belong
    and for the church in . . . .
May the good news be preached to the poor,
May the gospel be proclaimed in all places.
Lord, we need your help and your strength.
You come to rescue us.
Come, Lord our Saviour.

We remember before you the discouraged and fearful,
all whose freedom is limited by tyranny,
all whose lives are restricted by poverty,
all who are abused by those in power,
all whose dreams are destroyed by mockery.
You are the God who gives us hope.
You come to rescue us.
Come, Lord our Saviour.

We pray for the time when the lame will leap for joy,
when the deaf will hear,
when the blind will be able to see,
when the dumb will shout your praise,
when the handicapped will find freedom,
when sorrow and grief are done away
and all will sing and shout for joy.
We remember all who long for this time.
We pray for friends and loved ones in sickness,
we remember those who are terminally ill.
You are the God who gives us hope.

You come to rescue us.
Come, Lord our Saviour.

You are the Lord and giver of life,
you give life which is eternal.
We give you thanks for the saints in glory.
We remember before you all who have served this community
   in the past.
We remember loved ones departed this life.
You come to rescue us.
Come, Lord our Saviour.

THE PEACE

Tell everyone who is discouraged, 'Be strong, do not be afraid!
God is coming to your rescue.' The peace of the Lord be always
with you
and also with you.

THE BLESSING

Make a place for God in your hearts and in your lives, for he
comes to you this day and always; and the blessing of God
Almighty, the Father, the Son and the Holy Spirit, be upon you
and remain with you always. **Amen.**

The Fourth Sunday of Advent

———

Isaiah 7. 10–16 : Ps. 80. 1–7 [17–19] : Romans 1. 1–7 : Matthew 1. 18–25

King of kings yet born of Mary, you come to dwell among us in
great humility, you reveal the great love of God towards us and
that we are called to be his own people. Come now among us
and give us your peace, that we may live to your praise and
glory, Christ our Saviour, who is alive and lives and reigns with
the Father and the Spirit for ever and ever. **Amen**.

In the church that looks for you,
among the people who proclaim you,
with all who seek to serve you,
among all who dedicate their lives to you,
with all who proclaim that they love you,
now with us as we worship you,
with the church in . . . . and the church throughout
   the world,
Immanuel,
God, you are with us.

With the nations striving towards the light,
with the seekers for freedom and justice,
among those who enrich and extend our lives,
with all who bring peace on earth,
with the peoples lost in darkness,
with the nations caught up in war,
Immanuel,
God, you are with us.

In our homes as we prepare for your coming,
in our relationships and in our loving,
in our sharing and in our caring,
in our actions and our interactions,
now, within our community,
Immanuel,
God, you are with us.

With the outcasts and the poor,
with the unemployed and the homeless,
among the scorned and rejected,
with the refugees and the stateless,
with the persecuted and those who suffer injustice,
Immanuel,
God, you are with us.

With all who are in pain or sorrow,
With .... in their illness,
With .... in their anxiety,
with all who fear the future,
with those whose life on earth is coming to an end,
Immanuel,
God, you are with us.

With the whole church on earth,
with our loved ones at rest,
with the saints in glory,
Immanuel,
God, you are with us.

THE PEACE

From on high the Father has sent the Son to dwell among us
that we may know and share his peace.
The peace of the Lord be always with you
and also with you.

THE BLESSING

God is with you, a light to your path, a companion on the road, a friend for your journey, a sure support and presence at all times; and the blessing of God Almighty, the Father, the Son and the Holy Spirit, be upon you now and always. **Amen**.

Christmas

Christmas Day

Any of these sets of readings may be used on the evening of Christmas Eve and on Christmas Day.

I	II	III
Isaiah 9. 2–7	Isaiah 62. 6–12	Isaiah 52. 7–10
Ps. 96	Ps. 97	Ps. 98
Titus 2. 11–14	Titus 3. 4–7	Hebrews 1. 1–4 [5–12]
Luke 2. 1–14 [15–20]	Luke 2. [1–7] 8–20	John 1. 1–14

Lord Jesus Christ,
may we come to worship you with the shepherds,
proclaim you with the angels,
seek you with the wise men,
offer ourselves to you with Joseph and Mary,
and rejoice in your love, Christ our Lord,
who lives and reigns with the Father and the Spirit
    now and for ever. **Amen.**

Jesus, Son of Mary,
you have come among us, to be one of us.
We welcome you into our homes,
we welcome you into our hearts,
we welcome you into our lives.
Let all who come to your church, worship with the shepherds
and adore you with the wise men.

We pray for the time when the world may know
   your love and saving power.
Empower your church to show forth your glory.
Prince of peace,
reveal to us your glory.

The peace of your presence be upon your troubled world,
the power of your presence protect us from evil,
The light of your presence scatter the darkness from before us.
Give peace on earth, peace among the nations and
   peace in each land.
Prince of peace,
reveal to us your glory.

Fill us with wonder and awe,
fill us with joy and thanksgiving,
that our lives may proclaim your grace and your glory.
Be known in our homes,
in our lives and in all our dealings.
Prince of peace,
reveal to us your glory.

You could find no room at the inn.
We remember before you all who are homeless
   and can find no place of rest.
We pray for street children and children in care,
for all who are lonely and feel neglected this Christmas,
for those who will spend Christmas in hospital,
for all who are ill, especially . . . .
Prince of peace,
reveal to us your glory.

We rejoice that you became human that we might share in the
   Divine;
you came down to lift us into your kingdom.
We pray for all our loved ones departed
   and that we may share with them in a vision of your glory.

Prince of peace,
reveal to us your glory.

THE PEACE

Glory to God in the highest, and peace to people of goodwill.
The peace of the Lord be always with you
and also with you.

THE BLESSING

The wisdom of the Wonderful Counsellor guide you,
the strength of the Mighty God protect you,
the love of the Everlasting Father enfold you,
the peace of the Prince of peace be within you;
and the blessing...

The First Sunday of Christmas

———

Isaiah 63. 7–9 : Ps. 148. [1–6] 7–14 : Hebrews 2. 10–18 : Matthew 2. 13–23

Lord Jesus, born in a stable, sought by Herod, taken as a refugee to Egypt, hear the cry of all who are refugees and homeless. Fill us with love and care for them, and may we show that love in serving those in need. It is in serving them that we serve you, Jesus Christ our Lord. **Amen.**

Father, we remember before you all who are persecuted for
  their faith,
those imprisoned for their beliefs,
all who are forced out of their home and country
  for speaking out against evil and corruption.
We remember especially . . . .
Christ, be our Saviour.
By your presence save us.

We pray in sorrow for all innocent victims
  of tyranny and violence.
We pray for those who have suffered through ethnic cleansing
  or genocide.
We remember the people of . . . .
We pray for the refugees and displaced peoples.
We pray especially for . . . .
Christ, be our Saviour.
By your presence save us.

We give thanks to you for our homes.
We give thanks for our loved ones and our security.
We remember children in homes of abuse,
  children taken into care.
We pray for people evicted from their land or their homes,
for all who live in shanty towns or slum dwellings.
Christ, be our Saviour.
By your presence save us.

Lord, we remember all who have to leave home
  because of illness.
We pray for the handicapped,
for all who cannot cope on their own.
We remember all whose powers of mobility or agility are failing.
We pray for friends and loved ones in sickness,
  especially . . . .
Christ, be our Saviour.
By your presence save us.

Lord, we put our trust in you,
we believe that in you justice and love triumph.
We pray for all who are now departed from us,
    that they may rejoice in life eternal,
and that we may share with them in your everlasting kingdom.
Christ, be our Saviour.
By your presence save us.

THE PEACE

The peace of the Prince of peace fill your hearts and your minds;
and the peace of the Lord be always with you
and also with you.

THE BLESSING

Christ, the Son of God, born of Mary, fill you with his grace,
grant you a glimpse of his glory; and the blessing...

The Second Sunday of Christmas

———

Jeremiah 31. 7–14 : Ps. 147. 12–20 : *Or*: Ecclus. 24. 1–12 : *Canticle*: Wisdom of
Solomon 10. 15–21 : Ephesians 1. 3–14 : John 1. [1–9] 10–18

Almighty God, who through the coming of our Lord Jesus
Christ has caused a great light to shine in the darkness of our
world; grant that we may walk by that light, be known as
children of the light, and bring your light to the world; through

him who is the true light that lightens all, Jesus Christ our Lord.
Amen.

Holy Father, we pray that the church may proclaim your light
    in dark times,
that we may come to your light and recognize your light.
May we reach out to all who are in darkness.
May the church show forth the good news of the gospel.
We pray for all preachers of the word
    and ministers of sacraments,
for all who study the Scriptures.
We pray especially for . . . .
Christ, Light of the world,
scatter the darkness from before us.

We remember areas of the world where darkness seems to
    triumph,
places of exploitation and cheap labour,
places where the land is raped and forests are destroyed,
places where the water is polluted and the air is foul,
places where the sea is over-fished
    and the land is becoming desert.
We pray for ecologists and all who seek to care for our world.
We pray especially for . . . .
Christ, Light of the world,
scatter the darkness from before us.

We remember in sorrow broken relationships,
divisions in our community,
acts of selfishness and greed.
We pray for generosity of spirit,
for our homes and our loved ones.
Christ, Light of the world,
scatter the darkness from before us.

We pray for all who are in doubt and despair,
for all who have lost confidence in themselves or in others.

We pray for the depressed and all who walk in darkness.
We remember before you friends and loved ones in sickness.
We pray especially for..............
Christ, Light of the world,
scatter the darkness from before us.

We remember all who have passed through the darkness of
    death, and are alive with you in glory.
We give thanks for the saints
    and all who have shone out as lights in our world.
We pray for friends and loved ones who have enriched our lives
    and are now departed from us.
Christ, Light of the world,
scatter the darkness from before us.

THE PEACE

The light shines in the darkness, and the darkness cannot
    overcome it.
The peace of the Lord be always with you
and also with you.

THE BLESSING

Christ, the Light of the world, scatter the darkness from before
your path, that you may walk as children of the light. And the
blessing...

The Epiphany

The Epiphany

Isaiah 60. 1–6 : Ps. 72 [1–9] 10–15 : Ephesians 3. 1–12 : Matthew 2. 1–12

O God, who by the leading of a star revealed your Son to the nations of the world; lead us to a clearer vision of your presence, and the nations into the ways of unity and peace; through Jesus Christ our Lord. **Amen.**

As wise men from various nations were called to worship before
    the Christ child,
open our ears to your call,
and open our eyes to your glory.
We offer you all that we are, ourselves, our souls, our bodies.
We offer you all that we possess, for all things come from you.
We offer you our joys and our sorrows.
We pray for all seekers, for all who walk in the darkness and
    look for the light.
We pray for your church, that it may be drawn ever towards
    you.
Jesus, Light of the world,
give us your light and your peace.

Lord God, we pray that the rulers of this world may serve your
    kingdom,
that the kingdoms of the world may become
    the kingdom of Christ our Lord,

That the resources of the world may be used
  for the relief of those in need,
and to your praise and glory.
We remember all who are suffering from tyranny and violence,
  especially . . . .
Jesus, Light of the world,
give us your light and your peace.

We pray for all who work in our local communities,
for a sharing of talents and awareness of needs.
We thank you for the gifts you have given to us,
  and we seek to use them aright.
May our homes be places where the Christ abides
  and is always welcomed.
We remember all who have been driven out of their homes by
  poverty or war.
Jesus, Light of the world,
give us your light and your peace.

We pray for all who are in sorrow, pain or distress;
we remember especially . . . .
We pray for families where children are suffering,
  where children are ill.
We pray for children who suffer from violence, abuse or
  neglect.
We remember all who are struggling for justice and freedom.
Jesus, Light of the world,
give us your light and your peace.

We pray for all who have lost children,
for lives that have been cut short by accidents,
  by crime, or by illness;
may they have the fullness of life in your kingdom.
Give hope and strength to all parents who mourn,
  and bring a new light into their darkness.
Jesus, Light of the world,
give us your light and your peace.

Arise, shine out, for your light is come. The glory of the Lord is
   risen upon you.
The peace of the Lord be always with you
and also with you.

THE BLESSING

Christ be a bright flame before you, a guiding star above you, a
kindly shepherd behind you, a supporting strength beneath you;
and the blessing...

The Baptism of Christ
(The First Sunday of Epiphany)

———

Isaiah 42. 1–9 : Ps. 29 : Acts 10. 34–43 : Matthew 3. 13–17

Holy Father, who at the baptism of your beloved Son, revealed
his glory, grant us a glimpse of that glory in our lives; that we
may be ever immersed in your presence, Father, with the Son
and the Holy Spirit, one God for ever. **Amen.**

We give you thanks for our baptism,
   Creator, Redeemer and Sanctifier.
We give thanks for those who brought us to faith,
   who inspired us by word and example.
We pray for the outreach of the church,
for all who are unbaptized,

for all who have never heard the gospel clearly.
We pray for preachers, for prophets,
   for all who reveal your presence.
Lord, as we dwell in you,
may we know that you dwell in us.

We pray for all who are involved in providing us with our needs.
We pray for farmers and fishermen,
   for providers of food and security.
We pray for our police and ambulance service,
   for all who protect us.
Lord, as we dwell in you,
may we know that you dwell in us.

We remember before you our parents and our godparents.
We pray for our children and our godchildren.
We pray for the place where we were baptized.
We remember the people living along the river Jordan.
Lord, as we dwell in you,
may we know that you dwell in us.

Lord, we remember all who have lost vision,
all who have lost hope.
We pray for the despairing peoples of our world,
May they know that they abide in you and in your love.
We remember the lonely and the rejected.
We pray for all unwanted children,
   and the street children of our world.
We remember all who are in trouble or sickness,
   especially . . . .
Lord, as we dwell in you,
may we know that you dwell in us.

We rejoice that we have been baptized into your death and
   resurrection,
and we pray for all the faithful who have departed this life.

We remember the people of this church and community, especially . . . .
We pray that our loved ones may rejoice in the fullness of your presence.
Lord, as we dwell in you,
may we know that you dwell in us.

THE PEACE

The Lord shall give to his people the blessing of peace.
The peace of the Lord be always with you
and also with you.

THE BLESSING

The Father, who created you, calls you his beloved.
The Christ, who redeemed you, is with you in love.
The Spirit, who enlightens you, gives you strength.
The Holy Three are ever loving and guiding you.
And the blessing . . .

The Second Sunday of Epiphany

———

Isaiah 49. 1–7 : Ps. 40. 1–11 : 1 Corinthians 1. 1–9 : John 1. 29–42

O Lord our God, you call us in the depths of our being, you have a purpose for us: open our ears to your call, open our hearts to your love, open our minds to your purpose, that we may know you and give ourselves fully in your service, Father, Son and Holy Spirit. **Amen.**

Holy Three, we give thanks that you have called us.
You have called us to know you,
you have called us to love you,
you have called us to serve you.
Lord, make us worthy of our calling.
We pray for all who hear your call at this time,
    for all who seek to do your will.
We pray for those who have a vocation to the ordained
    ministry, and for lay ministers.
We pray for all who seek to bring others to you,
    for the whole mission of your church;
especially we pray for..............
Lord God, you call us to serve you.
Be our strength in all we do.

We give thanks for all who care for us in the service industries.
We pray for all who have been called to teach,
we pray for all who have been called to keep peace and order.
We pray especially for..............
Lord God, you call us to serve you.
Be our strength in all we do.

We give thanks for those who brought us to know you.
We pray for the faithful within our community,
that your grace and peace may be revealed in our homes.
We pray for our families and friends,
    especially those who still do not know you,
that we may be a good example and bring others to you.
Lord God, you call us to serve you.
Be our strength in all we do.

We pray for all who are called to the caring professions.
We pray for social workers, for home helps,
for doctors and nurses, for all who work in hospitals.

We remember all whose vocations are hindered by sickness or
   disability,
all whose lives are wasted through poverty and tyranny.
We remember all who are in trouble or sickness at this time,
   especially . . . .
Lord God, you call us to serve you.
Be our strength in all we do.

We give thanks for all who have served you faithfully
   and are now at rest,
all who are called to be saints.
We pray for our dear ones who are departed from us.
Lord God, you call us to serve you.
Be our strength in all we do.

THE PEACE

Grace to you, and peace from God our Father and the Lord
   Jesus Christ.
The peace of the Lord be always with you
and also with you.

THE BLESSING

The Lord God who has called you into being and called you
into his service, give you strength to do all that he would have
you do, and make you worthy of your calling; and the
blessing . . .

The Third Sunday of Epiphany

Isaiah 9. 1–4 : Ps. 27. 1 [2–3] 4–9 : 1 Corinthians 1. 10–18 : Matthew 4. 12–23

Lord God, you are almighty; in your great power renew, refresh, restore us, that we may live and work to your praise and glory; through Jesus Christ our Lord who is alive and reigns with you, O Father, and the Holy Spirit, for ever and ever. **Amen.**

Lord, be a light to our path, and a strength for our journey.
When we call, have mercy and answer us.
May we hear and heed your call,
 that we may walk as children of light.
May we leave the trivial things of this world
 to come to behold your glory.
As the disciples were called to be fishers of men,
 keep us true to your gospel.
May we seek to bring others to you.
We pray for evangelists and preachers,
for Sunday school teachers, and leaders of study groups.
Especially we pray for . . . .
Lord, our light and our salvation,
Lord, be the strength of our life.

Shine in the dark places of our world,
 that there may be hope and light.
We pray for impoverished peoples,
those who have suffered from natural disasters,

those who have suffered through the greed of others or through
   war.
We remember all whose freedom is limited,
   whose lives are darkened by cruelty.
Lord, our light and our salvation.
Lord, be the strength of our life.

Lord, with you is the well of life,
   and in your light we shall see life.
We give thanks for our parents.
We pray for our families and loved ones,
for our places of work and the communities to which we
   belong.
Lord, our light and our salvation,
Lord, be the strength of our life.

We pray for those who feel lost, without vocation or purpose.
We remember the unemployed, the redundant,
   the severely handicapped.
We remember the world poor and the hungry.
We pray for all who are in sickness, especially . . . .
Scatter the gloom from all who are in anguish.
Lord, our light and our salvation,
Lord, be the strength of our life.

We give thanks for all who have served you faithfully,
for those who have enriched the world by their goodness,
for the well known and those who were never noticed except by
   you;
may they continue to serve you in glory.
Lord, our light and our salvation.
Lord, be the strength of our life.

THE PEACE

The joy of the Lord be your strength, the love of the Lord your
peace; and the peace of the Lord be always with you
and also with you.

THE BLESSING

The almighty Father be your strength,
The gracious Lord be your support,
The generous Spirit protect you;
and the blessing...

The Fourth Sunday of Epiphany

---

1 Kings 17. 8–16 : Ps. 36. 5–10 : 1 Corinthians 1. 18–31 : John 2. 1–11

Lord of all power and might, giver of strength and joy,
transform the poverty of our nature into the riches of your
glory; that, in changing us, your grace and goodness may be
revealed, through Jesus Christ our Lord. **Amen.**

Lord, there are times when life can run out of its resources,
times when life can be dull and dreary.
Lord, when our resources run dry,
by your love, transform us.

We pray for a church often appearing old and dry,
a church that can be rigid in practice, unbending in attitude,
a church lacking in gifts, failing to bring light and joy,

31

seemingly running out of the richness of the gospel.
Lord, when our resources run dry,
by your love, transform us.

We pray for our ever-changing world,
a world often depleted of energy, running short of vision,
a world misusing its resources.
We pray for the rain forests,
for lands where the desert is increasing,
for all impoverished peoples.
Lord, when our resources run dry,
by your love, transform us.

We pray for homes that are caught up in dull routines,
for homes that are not life-giving or life-restoring.
We pray for those who are exhausted in caring for others.
Lord, when our resources run dry,
by your love, transform us.

We remember before you the world-weary,
all who find life dull and dreary,
   all whose lives lack sparkle and spirit.
We remember the despairing and the depressed,
all who are worn out, who have run out of energy.
Lord, when our resources run dry,
by your love, transform us.

We think of the time when all resources run out,
when the heart stops and life ceases.
We rejoice that you are the Lord who restores and redeems.
You give us life which is eternal.
We remember loved ones departed, especially . . . .
Lord, when our resources run dry,
by your love, transform us.

THE PEACE

They that wait upon the Lord shall renew their strength.
The peace of the Lord be always with you
and also with you.

THE BLESSING

The Holy and Strong One, the Holy and Mighty One, grant you renewal, restoration and his power for the days to come. And the blessing...

Ordinary Time

Proper 1

Sunday between 3 and 9 February inclusive
(if earlier than the Second Sunday before Lent)

Isaiah 58. 1–9a [b–12] : Ps. 112. 1–9 [10] : 1 Corinthians 2.1–12 [13–16] :
Matthew 5. 13–20

God of grace, God of glory,
guide us by your goodness,
that we may walk in your ways,
seek to do your will, and worship you always;
through Jesus Christ our Lord,
who is alive and reigns with you and the Holy Spirit,
one God, now and for ever. **Amen.**

We give thanks to you, O Father,
for the light that shines in our lives through Christ our Lord.
Fill your church with that light,
that it may be a light to light all nations,
that we may proclaim your presence and your glory.
We pray for all visionaries,
for all who patiently wait upon you.
We pray for all who have dedicated their lives to you,
for all who work in your church today.
We remember especially those who have served you faithfully
    for many years.

We pray for the growth of the church in our generation.
Light of Christ,
scatter the darkness from your world.

We pray for the nations who have difficult decisions to make
    and are not sure which way to turn.
We pray for all who strive to bring in justice,
to free the oppressed,
to share with the hungry,
to house the homeless and to care for the poor.
We pray for leaders who feel they are working in the dark,
for all who cannot find answers to the problems before them.
Light of Christ,
scatter the darkness from your world.

We pray that the dark places of our hearts, and all dark deeds,
    will be done away.
That the darkness may be dispersed from our communities,
that sin and vice, greed and violence may be done away,
that our homes may be places of peace and light.
Light of Christ,
scatter the darkness from your world.

We pray that all who walk in darkness and in the shadow of
    death may see your light.
We remember all who have lost hope,
all who have ceased to trust.
We pray for all captives,
for the hungry and the homeless.
We pray for all who are in sickness, especially . . . .
May your healing be known among them.
Light of Christ,
scatter the darkness from your world.

We give thanks that life is eternal.
We remember loved ones who have gone before us
    and are in the fullness of light in your kingdom.

We pray that one day we may all walk in that light.
Light of Christ,
scatter the darkness from your world.

The light of Christ scatter the darkness from before your path;
and the peace of the Lord be always with you
and also with you

Christ, the Son of Glory, shine upon you, that you may walk in
the light as in the day, and not in the night; and the blessing...

Proper 2

*Sunday between 10 and 16 February inclusive
(if earlier than the Second Sunday before Lent)*

———

Deuteronomy 30. 15–20 *or* Ecclesiasticus 15. 15–20 : Ps. 119. 1–8 :
1 Corinthians 3. 1–9 : Matthew 5. 21–37

Enfold us, Lord, in your love,
surround us with your peace,
encircle us with your power.
Enable us to be what you would have us be;
empower us to do what you would have us do;
through Christ our living Lord. **Amen.**

Lord, as you are generous to us, may we be generous to others.
Lord, as you forgive us, may we learn to forgive others.
You give us life, you give us love, you give us yourself;
let us give our lives, our love, ourselves, to you.
Help us to choose the way of life and to lead others
    to him who is the Way the Truth and the Life.
May your church be an example of discipline and discipleship.
Help us to rejoice in life, and to work together
    for the building up of your kingdom.
Life-giving God,
hear us and be with us.

May your world work for the ways that lead to peace,
that there may be peace and goodwill among the nations,
that the resources of the world may be respected and cared for,
that all who work for the prosperity of the world may be
    encouraged.
We remember all who work for renewal and restoration in
    derelict areas.
Life-giving God,
hear us and be with us.

We pray that discord and anger may be taken away from our
    hearts and our communities,
that broken relationships may find healing,
that communities may turn to the ways of peace and trust,
that the destructive forces within us may be conquered.
Life-giving God,
hear us and be with us.

We pray for all who are facing disaster or destruction,
all whose land is being destroyed by greed,
all whose lives are being destroyed by choosing ways that lead
    to death.
We pray for all drug addicts,
    all whose lives are marred by their past,
and all whose lives are diminished by sickness.

Life-giving God,
hear us and be with us.

We rejoice that nothing can separate us from the love of God in
   Christ Jesus.
We pray for all who have passed through death,
   especially . . . .
Life-giving God,
hear us and be with us.

THE PEACE

Love the Lord your God, obey him, hold fast to him, for that
means life to you, and peace; and the peace of the Lord be
always with you
and also with you.

THE BLESSING

God, the creator of life, is with you.
Christ, the Way the Truth and the Life, is with you.
The Holy Spirit, the Lord and giver of life, is with you.
And the blessing . . .

Proper 3

Sunday between 17 and 23 February inclusive
(if earlier than the Second Sunday before Lent)

Leviticus 19. 1–2, 9–18 : Ps. 119. 33–40 : 1 Corinthians 3. 10–11, 16–23 :
Matthew 5. 38–48

Lord, in the clouds and darkness of this world, grant us a
glimpse of your glory, that we may set ourselves to share in the
bringing in of your kingdom. As you refresh and restore us, may
we work for the renewal of your world; through Christ our
Lord, who is alive and reigns with you and the life-giving Spirit,
for ever and ever. **Amen.**

Father, make us holy as you are holy,
    that we may belong to you.
Turn our eyes from watching what is worthless,
    to behold your glory.
Let your church show that the Spirit of God is within us,
that we belong to Christ and to you.
We pray that your church will grow in holiness,
    in outreach and in number.
God, give us grace
to build on sure foundations.

We pray for the harvests of your world,
that they may not be hoarded or squandered,
that the land may be respected and cared for,
that no people may hunger or be misused by others.
We remember nations or individuals who are deeply in debt.

We pray for all who have lost their freedom or their livelihood.
God, give us grace
to build on sure foundations.

We pray for our homes and our loved ones,
that enmity and strife in our communities may be conquered,
that forgiveness and mutual respect may be part of our lives.
We pray for the renewal of broken relationships, and broken
    hearts.
God, give us grace
to build on sure foundations.

We remember all who have suffered from fraud,
    from robbery, from low wages,
all who have suffered through injustice,
all who have been slandered or maligned,
all who have suffered mockery and scorn.
We remember all whose lives are crumbling around them.
God, give us grace
to build on sure foundations.

That we may endure all,
    and come at last to your glorious kingdom,
that we may share with our loved ones in glory,
God, give us grace
to build on sure foundations.

THE PEACE

You are the temple of God; God's Holy Spirit dwells within you.
The peace of the Lord be always with you
and also with you.

THE BLESSING

Love your enemies, pray for those that persecute you, so that you
may be children of your Father in heaven; and the blessing...

The Second Sunday Before Lent

Genesis 1.1—2.3 : Ps. 136 or Ps. 136. 1–9, 23–26 : Romans 8. 18–25 :
Matthew 6. 25–34

Lord God, you have made us in your image;
may we show forth your glory in our lives
and lead others to an awareness of you,
through Christ our Lord,
who with you, O Father, and the Holy Spirit,
reigns supreme for ever and ever. **Amen.**

Good and glorious God, we thank you for all your gifts in
    creation.
We give thanks for the wonder and the beauty of the world.
Help us to love the world with the great love which you have
    for the world.
Grant your church to order its priorities,
that above all things we may seek you and your kingdom, that
    we may show forth your love, and your care for all.
We pray for all who reach out in mission,
for the growth of your church,
for its worship and its ministry.
Lord, your kingdom come
on earth as it is in heaven.

We pray for areas of the world that are marred by greed and
    war,
for all people who live in slums and bad housing,
for the unemployed and the redundant,

for all street children and those who are unwanted.
Lord, your kingdom come
on earth as it is in heaven.

That our homes may be places of peace and love,
that our lives may reflect your love and acceptance,
that our communities may show your beauty and joy,
Lord, your kingdom come
on earth as it is in heaven.

We pray for all who are worried about where their next meal
    comes from,
the hungry and ill-clad of our world,
those whose barns are empty,
all who worry about what tomorrow will bring.
We pray for the anxious, the fearful, the troubled,
that they may find your love and your peace.
Lord, your kingdom come
on earth as it is in heaven.

We remember all who are now delivered from the troubles of
    this world and are at peace,
all whose time of fear and anxiety is over and are at rest.
Lord, your kingdom come
on earth as it is in heaven.

THE PEACE

The God of hope fill you with all joy and peace in believing; and
the peace of the Lord be always with you
and also with you.

THE BLESSING

Do not worry about your life, what you will eat or what you will
drink, or about your body what you will wear; your heavenly
Father knows that you need all these things. And the blessing . . .

The Sunday Next Before Lent

Exodus 24. 12–18 : Ps. 2 *or* Ps. 99 : 2 Peter 1. 16–21 : Matthew 17. 1–9

Lord, change us and we shall be changed,
transform us by your love,
redeem us by your grace,
strengthen us by your presence,
that we may move from glory to glory;
through Christ our Lord, who with the Holy Spirit
reigns with you, O Father, in glory everlasting. **Amen.**

Lord, bless your church that it may reflect your glory,
that it may guide your people into the ways of love and peace.
We pray for the church as it seeks to uphold your law and to
  discover your will,
that we may be faithful to you
  until the day dawns and the morning star rises in our hearts.
Lord, enable us to proclaim your kingdom and your glory.
Good and gracious God,
grant us a glimpse of your glory.

We pray for a world that so often has lost its way,
a world without standards, without direction.
We pray for all whose life has no purpose or meaning,
for all who are confused and needing guidance.
Good and gracious God,
grant us a glimpse of your glory.

Good Lord, transform our lives by a vision of your glory.
Transform our work by an awareness of your presence.
Transform our homes by a knowledge of your love.
Transform our relationships by our being with you.
Good and gracious God,
grant us a glimpse of your glory.

Good Lord, transform our hospitals by your power,
transform our fears by your love,
transform our darkness by your light.
We remember before you all who need your transforming
     power, especially..............
Good and gracious God,
grant us a glimpse of your glory.

Lord, transform our fear of death by our knowing you.
We remember before you loved ones already transformed in
     likeness to your glory.
Good and gracious God,
grant us a glimpse of your glory.

THE PEACE

God, who has the power to give us peace and fill our lives with
glory, is with us now.
The peace of the Lord be always with you
and also with you.

THE BLESSING

God, who gives us glory,
make you holy in every way,
and keep you from the powers of evil;
and the blessing...

Lent

The First Sunday of Lent

Genesis 2. 15–17; 3. 1–7 : Ps. 32 : Romans 5. 12–19 : Matthew 4. 1–11

Almighty God,
Give us grace to cast away the works of darkness,
cleanse and deliver us from all our sins,
confirm and strengthen us in all goodness,
and bring us into the way that leads to life;
through him who is the Way the Truth and the Life,
Jesus Christ our Lord. **Amen.**

Lord, we remember in your presence the sins of your church.
We fail to live up to our ideals,
we compromise for comfort,
we are often too concerned about material things,
we seek our own glory.
We do not put our trust in you,
   but trust in our own schemes and plans, in our own strength.
Lord, help us to see our priorities,
and not to be led astray.
Lord, lead us from temptation
and deliver us from evil.

Lord, we belong to a fallen world,
   where your image is marred and your creation despoiled.

We seek quick and cheap results
   and disregard the consequences.
The air is polluted and our rivers foul,
our land is raped through greed.
Help all who seek to redeem this world
   and to save it from destruction.
Give vision to world leaders
and to all who are in control of our industries.
Lord lead us from temptation
and deliver us from evil.

Lord, make us aware of the wonder and the beauty that is about
   us.
Help us to move towards a better environment.
We pray for our homes and all that goes on in them.
We pray for our relationships with each other.
We pray especially for all who have found a loved one
   unfaithful.
Lord, lead us from temptation
and deliver us from evil.

We remember all who have suffered through their sinfulness,
all who are caught up in vice or crime,
all who are drug addicts,
all who have been misused or abused by others,
all who live below their abilities and ideals,
all who are tempted to despair, all who are suicidal.
Lord, lead us from temptation
and deliver us from evil.

We rejoice with all who have triumphed over sin and death.
We give thanks for all who have given us a good example to
   follow,
for all who know the forgiveness of sins
   and the gift of eternal life.
May we share with them in your kingdom.

Lord, lead us from temptation
and deliver us from evil.

THE PEACE

Be glad, you righteous, rejoice in the Lord; shout for joy all that
are true of heart; and the peace of the Lord be always with you
and also with you.

THE BLESSING

The good and gracious God deliver you from all that is evil,
confirm and strengthen you in all goodness; and the blessing of
God . . .

The Second Sunday of Lent

Genesis 12. 1–4a : Ps. 121 : Romans 4. 1–5, 13–17 : John 3. 1–17

Lord God, you have created us for yourself,
you have called us into being,
you have offered us your love.
We give ourselves, our souls and bodies,
and all that we do, to you in love;
through our Saviour Christ our Lord. **Amen.**

Lord, increase our faith that we may trust in you.
May we move forward knowing that you are with us and before
us.

Give us a vision of who we are and what we should do.
Help us to move towards your promised land.
May your church work for the freedom of captives,
for the release of those unjustly bound,
for a more caring and peaceful world.
Our help comes from the Lord,
the maker of heaven and earth.

Lord, teach us to love the world
   with the great love that you have for the world.
Guide all leaders of peoples,
strengthen the good,
lead us in ways of peace.
Grant sensitivity to planners and to all who affect our future.
We pray for research workers and inventors,
for all who influence our lives and minds,
that our world may be kept in goodness and in beauty.
Our help comes from the Lord,
the maker of heaven and earth.

We remember all who are fearful of the future.
We pray for those who are seriously or terminally ill,
for all who await a doctor's diagnosis,
all who await operations or treatment.
We ask you to strengthen all who are despairing,
to encourage and hearten all who have lost hope.
Our help comes from the Lord,
the maker of heaven and earth.

We give thanks for all who have passed through death
   and reached the fullness of the promised land.
We rejoice in their fellowship and their triumph.
We offer ourselves, our neighbours and our loved ones to your
   unfailing love.
Our help comes from the Lord,
the maker of heaven and earth.

Just as Moses lifted up the serpent in the wilderness, so must the Son of Man be lifted up, that whoever believes in him may have eternal life.
The peace of the Lord be always with you
and also with you.

THE BLESSING

Everyone that believes in him shall not perish, but have everlasting life. The blessing of God . . .

The Third Sunday of Lent

Exodus 17. 1–7 ː Ps. 95 ː Romans 5. 1–11 ː John 4. 5–42

Eternal God and Father,
we thirst for your love,
we long for your presence,
we yearn for your peace.
Come, Lord, restore us that we may live to your glory;
through him who gives us the water of life,
Jesus Christ our Lord. **Amen.**

Lord, as we journey towards the promised land,
refresh, renew, restore us in your service.
We pray for churches where life has become dull and dry.
We remember churches struggling for survival.

We pray for Christians drained of energy and resources.
We remember especially those who thirst for your presence and
    your saving power.
Good and gracious Lord,
give us the water of life.

We pray for all who thirst after justice,
all who are working hard to improve our world.
We remember all who are suffering from weariness and
    exhaustion.
We pray for all who live in desert lands.
Good and gracious Lord,
give us the water of life.

We pray for all who are going through a period of testing and
    dryness, in their faith or their relationships.
We pray for those whose ardour has cooled,
for all who have lost their first zeal and zest for life.
We pray for all who are suffering from a lack of love in their
    homes.
Good and gracious Lord,
give us the water of life.

We remember all who feel wrung out or dried up,
all who are wearied with the journey of life,
all who feel they are near to perishing.
We pray for all who cannot cope by themselves,
for all who are in care, and for all carers.
We remember all who are in a hospice.
Good and gracious Lord,
give us the water of life.

We give thanks for the fellowship of those whose journey is over,
those who hunger and thirst no more,
all who have been refreshed and restored in your kingdom.
We pray that we may share with them in the fullness of life
    which is eternal.

Good and gracious Lord,
give us the water of life.

The Lord keeps in perfect peace all who have their minds stayed
   on him.
The peace of the Lord be always with you
and also with you.

The almighty Father refresh you,
The loving Saviour redeem you,
The life-giving Spirit restore you;
and the blessing...

The Fourth Sunday of Lent

1 Samuel 16. 1–13 : Ps. 23 : Ephesians 5. 8–14 : John 9. 1–41

Lord, open our eyes to your presence,
open our ears to your call,
open our hearts to your love;
that we may give ourselves to you
and walk before you as children of light;
through him who is the Light of the World,
Jesus Christ our Lord. **Amen.**

Father, creator of light,
we remember all who walk in darkness,
all who do not know your love,
all who are unaware of your light.
We pray that your church may shine as a light in the world
and bring all peoples to you who are the true light.
We pray for all who go out in mission,
all who proclaim your love.
Jesus, Light of the world,
scatter the darkness from our hearts and minds.

We pray for all who are caught up in works of darkness,
those who misuse your world,
those who have no respect for people or their feelings,
those who deal in wickedness and vice;
that a new awareness may conquer their blindness,
a new vision dispel their darkness.
Jesus, Light of the world,
scatter the darkness from our hearts and minds.

Lord, forgive the hurt we cause by our own blindness.
May the brightness of your light bring joy to our homes,
new love to our relationships,
deep peace to our communities.
Jesus, Light of the world,
scatter the darkness from our hearts and minds.

We pray for all who are blind, for all whose sight is failing.
We remember all whose minds are darkened by fear or sin,
all who are beset by dark deeds of the past.
We pray for the healing of the past
    in our lives and our communities.
We pray for all who are consumed by hatred
    or by desire for revenge.
Jesus, Light of the world,
scatter the darkness from our hearts and minds.

We praise you for all who have entered into a fuller vision,
all who have awakened to your glory in heaven.
We pray that we may not sorrow for the departed
  but rejoice in their freedom.
Jesus, Light of the world,
scatter the darkness from our hearts and minds.

THE PEACE

Walk in his light, that you may become children of light.
The peace of the Lord be always with you
and also with you.

THE BLESSING

May the Christ who has conquered the darkness, bring light
and joy to your life; and the blessing...

*The Fifth Sunday of Lent
(Passiontide begins)*

Ezekiel 37. 1–14 : Ps. 130 : Romans 8. 6–11 : John 11. 1–45

Holy Father, you have challenged the powers of darkness,
through your Son, and have committed your church to share in
your redeeming works; grant that we, who bear witness to your
saving power in words, may do so in deeds; through him who

died for us and rose again, Jesus Christ our Lord, who with you
and the Holy Spirit is one God for ever and ever. **Amen.**

Come, Lord, like the wind, move us, direct us.
Come as the breath, fill us, refresh us.
Come to your church which without you is dull and dry, and fill
  us with your Spirit.
Call us out of death and darkness into life and light.
We pray for the renewal of your church in its devotion and
  mission,
for all who proclaim your life-giving powers
  and share in your redeeming love.
Come, Lord, restore, renew,
revive your people.

We pray for all whose hope is lost, who feel cut off from life,
for refugees and displaced peoples,
for all who flee from oppression and tyranny,
for all who are made homeless,
for all who have suffered abuse or violence.
Come, Lord, restore, renew,
revive your people.

We pray for areas of bad housing
where communities have broken down or have died.
We pray for friends and loved ones who are worn out,
for relationships that are in danger of dying.
Come, Lord, restore, renew,
revive your people.

We pray for all who are ill,
for all who are in weakness,
for all who are bereaved.
We remember all who have given up on life.
We pray for the disturbed, for the mentally ill,
for all who walk in darkness and in the shadow of death.
We pray for all who suffer torture or violence.

Come, Lord, restore, renew,
revive your people.

We give thanks for all who set us an example of love
and vitality and who have now entered your greater glory.
May we be inspired by their lives
and seek to live to your praise and glory.
Come, Lord, restore, renew,
revive your people.

THE PEACE

He who raised Jesus from the dead, will give life to your mortal
bodies.
The peace of the Lord be always with you
and also with you.

THE BLESSING

May you find in Christ crucified
a strength in times of darkness,
a support in times of weakness,
and the assurance that life is eternal;
and the blessing of God...

Palm Sunday (Liturgy of the Passion)

Isaiah 50. 4–9a : Ps. 31. 9–16 [17–18] : Philippians 2. 5–11 :
Matthew 26.14—27.66 *or* Matthew 27. 11–54

Lord, you give us life, you give us love, you give us yourself:
help us to give our lives, our love, ourselves to you; through
Christ who died and rose again for us and who lives with you
and the Holy Spirit in everlasting light. **Amen.**

Lord, we come to you as a church broken by sin, divided by
    factions.
We come weak in our mission, failing in holiness.
We come neglectful in our prayers and insensitive to your
    presence.
We come lacking in vision, wavering in faith.
We remember all who have broken faith,
broken vows, broken commitments.
Lord, broken on the cross, we come to you.
Only you can make us whole.

We come with people broken by war,
with all divided by fear,
with all who are shattered by betrayal of trust,
with all who are fractured by oppression.
Lord, broken on the cross, we come to you.
Only you can make us whole.

Lord, we come with broken hopes and broken dreams,
with broken relationships and broken hearts,

with broken promises and broken trust.
We come as shattered people.
Lord, broken on the cross, we come to you.
Only you can make us whole.

We come with all your broken people.
We come with the broken in spirit,
with the despondent and the despairing.
We come with the broken in mind,
with the deeply distressed and the disturbed.
We come with the broken in body,
with all who are injured and all who are ill.
We come to you with all our needs.
Lord, broken on the cross, we come to you.
Only you can make us whole.

We remember all who have been killed through injustice,
    cruelty or carelessness,
all who have died that others might live.
We rejoice that now they know the wholeness and
    holiness of your kingdom.
Lord, broken on the cross, we come to you.
Only you can make us whole.

THE PEACE

The Lord God is your helper; he who vindicates you is near.
The peace of the Lord be always with you
and also with you.

THE BLESSING

Do not be afraid, stand firm, know the saving power of God;
and the blessing . . .

57

Easter

Easter Day

Acts 10. 34–43 *or* Jeremiah 31. 1–6 : Ps. 118. [1–2] 14–24 : Colossians 3. 1–4
or Acts 10. 34–43 : John 20. 1–18 *or* Matthew 28. 1–10

Alleluia to our God, praise and thanksgiving for life and life
    eternal.
Alleluia to our Lord Jesus Christ, conqueror of death and hell.
Alleluia to Christ, the gateway to life everlasting.
Father, Son and Holy Spirit,
we praise you for your life-giving and life-renewing powers,
this glorious day and evermore. **Amen.**

Blessed are you, Lord God our Father,
by whose power our Lord Jesus Christ is risen from the dead.
We rejoice and celebrate that he who was dead is alive,
that he who was buried is risen.
Death is conquered, we are free,
    Christ has won the victory.
Lord, make us aware of the presence of the Risen Christ in our
    lives.
Let the church proclaim the good news, 'He is risen!'
In the power of the risen Lord, let us lead people out of
    darkness into light.
Christ Jesus, risen in glory,
scatter the darkness from our hearts and from your world.

Lord Jesus, as we rejoice this day,
we remember your words to the disciples,
  'Peace be unto you'.
We pray for peace in our world,
that we may rise above all that would cause strife and conflict,
that your victory over the powers of evil may be allowed to
  work in your world.
Christ Jesus, risen in glory,
scatter the darkness from our hearts and from your world.

Risen Lord, as you appeared to Mary in the garden,
  to the disciples in the Upper Room,
  to the travellers on the road to Emmaus,
be known among us.
Christ be in our homes, in our work and in our journeying.
Risen Lord, let us walk in your presence and peace.
Christ Jesus, risen in glory,
scatter the darkness from our hearts and from your world.

We remember before you all who walk in darkness and fear,
all who are weighed down, all who are heavily laden.
We pray for all who have lost hope,
for all who are approaching death,
for those caring for the terminally ill,
for those in a hospice.
Christ Jesus, risen in glory,
scatter the darkness from our hearts and from your world.

We rejoice in the glory of the our Risen Lord
and of all your saints who have shared in your triumph over the
  grave and death.
We pray today for our loved ones departed,
that they may rejoice in the glory of your presence.
Christ Jesus, risen in glory,
scatter the darkness from our hearts and from your world.

Glory, glory, glory to Christ our risen Lord, who reigns with the Father and the Holy Spirit for ever. Peace through our Lord Jesus Christ, he is Lord of life and death; he is Lord of all. The peace of the Lord be always with you
and also with you.

THE BLESSING

May you find in Christ Jesus, our risen Lord, a companion for your journey, a sure ground for your hopes, the peace that passes understanding, and the joy that life is eternal; and the blessing . . .

The Second Sunday of Easter

Acts 2. 14a, 22–32 : Ps. 16 : 1 Peter 1. 3–9 : John 20. 19–31

Blessing and praise be to you, Lord our God and Father of our
    Lord Jesus Christ!
By your great mercy you have given us new life and new hope
through the resurrection of our Lord Jesus Christ from the
    dead.
You have brought us into an inheritance
that is imperishable, undefiled and unfading and in heaven.
To you be praise, through Christ our Risen Lord,
who is alive and reigns with you and the Holy Spirit,
one God now and for ever. **Amen.**

Lord, we give thanks for all who, though they have not seen
   you, have believed.
We give thanks for the disciples and your appearing to them in
   the Upper Room.
Help us to know that you are with us in your risen power.
We pray for Christians who are fearful of persecution,
for all who are suffering because of their faith.
May your church speak out boldly
   in the power of your resurrection.
Christ, risen Lord, be with us
and give us your peace.

We pray for all who are seekers after justice,
   freedom and peace.
Bless the work of the United Nations
   and all peace-keeping forces.
Protect all who seek to bring new life and peace
   to troubled communities.
We pray for community workers and all local councils.
Christ, risen Lord, be with us
and give us your peace.

We give thanks for those who taught us the faith,
   who shared their beliefs with us.
We are grateful for all who have set us examples to follow.
May we rejoice in your presence in our homes.
May we show forth your power in our lives.
Bless us in all our dealings and relationships.
Christ, risen Lord, be with us
and give us your peace.

We pray for all who are locked in by guilt or fear,
all who are afraid to venture because of risk and danger.
We pray for all who need healing of past hurts,
   for the healing of memories,
for all who are suffering from losing loved ones
   through accidents, crime, or illness.

Christ, risen Lord, be with us
and give us your peace.

We give thanks for all who have passed beyond death and
   rejoice in your kingdom,
for all who have triumphed over sin and suffering
   and are now at peace.
Christ, risen Lord, be with us
and give us your peace.

THE PEACE

Even though you do not see him now, you believe in him and
rejoice with an indescribable and glorious joy, for you are
receiving the outcome of your faith, the salvation of your souls.
The peace of the Lord be always with you
and also with you.

THE BLESSING

Fix your gaze on the glory of the risen Lord, and be transformed
by him from glory to glory; and the blessing...

The Third Sunday of Easter

Acts 2. 14a, 36–41 : Ps. 116. 1–4, 12–19 (or 1–8) : 1 Peter 1. 17–23 :
Luke 24. 13–35

Abide with us Lord, throughout this day.
Abide with us in our journeying, and in our homes.
Abide with us in our seeking and in our longings.
Abide with us now and to eternity,
Jesus, risen Lord, who lives and reigns with the Father and the
  Holy Spirit
in glory for ever. **Amen.**

Lord, that we may know you in the breaking,
in the break of day, in the breaking of hearts,
and in the breaking of bread,
help us to know that you are risen indeed,
and that you are with us in the holy communion.
May your church ever proclaim your presence,
and know that you travel with us on the road we go.
Teach us, Lord, to abide in you,
    that we may know you abide in us.
We pray that your church will walk with the downcast, the
  seekers, the troubled in heart,
and help to reveal your love and presence.
Lord, abide with us
and we will abide in you.

We pray today for all who journey,
for those who are leaving places of pain and sorrow,

for those whose lives may be in danger,
for all pilgrims and seekers,
for refugees and homeless people,
for all who travel by land, sea or air,
    and for all who have the care of them.
Lord, abide with us
and we will abide in you.

We give thanks that you come to us.
Make us aware of your presence in our homes.
Help us to be aware of you as our hearts burn within us.
Help us to see you, O Christ, in everyone we meet.
We pray for the lonely, for all who feel rejected,
    for the outcasts of society.
Lord, abide with us
and we will abide in you.

We pray for the broken-hearted,
for those whose hopes have died,
for all who are confused by the pain and sickness of our world.
We remember all who travel by lonely paths,
all who are coming to the end of their journey in this world and
    walk towards the sunset.
We pray for the elderly,
for all who are in care,
for all who cannot cope on their own.
Lord, abide with us
and we will abide in you.

We pray for all who have been killed in road accidents,
for all who have come to an untimely end.
We pray that you will protect us in our journey,
until we share with the saints in your kingdom.
Lord, abide with us
and we will abide in you.

THE PEACE

You have been born anew, not of perishable but of imperishable
seed, through the living and enduring word of God.
The peace of the Lord be always with you
and also with you.

THE BLESSING

Abide in Christ as he abides in you, and he will raise you up at
the last day; and the blessing...

The Fourth Sunday of Easter

Acts 2. 42–47 : Ps. 23 : 1 Peter 2. 19–25 : John 10. 1–10

Glory to you O Lord!
You have triumphed over the powers of darkness
and brought us to share in the inheritance of your saints in light.
Raise us up to newness of life,
that we may live to serve you, risen Lord,
who with the Father and the life-giving Spirit
are one God, world without end. **Amen.**

Father, we give you thanks for the church,
for its teaching and fellowship,
for the breaking of the bread together and for prayer.
We pray that we may always come before you with reverence
and awe.

We give you thanks for faithful stewardship,
   for all who care and share.
May your church use its possessions aright,
   to the relief of the needy and to your praise and glory.
Give us glad and generous hearts.
Let us seek out and rescue the lost and the straying,
protect the young, and uplift any who are fallen.
Good Shepherd,
guide us and lead us.

We pray for all who walk in darkness
   and in the valley of the shadow of death.
We remember all who are caught up in strife and warfare,
all areas of great poverty,
all areas of decadence and evil,
all places where we have spoiled the environment.
We pray that we may find ways that lead to joy
   and life in all its fullness.
Good Shepherd,
guide us and lead us.

Lord, as you have opened for us the gate of everlasting life,
help us to live life to the full.
May we help others to extend their lives and their vision.
Bless our homes and our loved ones with the fullness of life.
Make us useful members of the communities to which we
   belong.
Good Shepherd,
guide us and lead us.

We remember before you all whose lives are restricted.
We pray for the handicapped, the deaf, the dumb and the blind,
for all whose lives are impaired through the cruelty or neglect of
   others.
We pray for all who are in sickness.
We pray that we may help where we can.

Good Shepherd,
guide us and lead us.

Lord, you open the gate of glory
that we may see the joy before us.
We give thanks for all who have triumphed over their
limitations and now have life in all its fullness.
We pray especially for . . . .
Good Shepherd,
guide us and lead us.

THE PEACE

Trust God, who raises the dead, to save you from mortal
danger. Put all your hope in him.
The peace of the Lord be always with you
and also with you.

THE BLESSING

Christ, that great Shepherd of the sheep, who has opened for
you the gate of glory, give you life in all its fullness and lead you
to life eternal; and the blessing . . .

The Fifth Sunday of Easter

Acts 7. 55–60 : Ps. 31. 1–5 [15–16] : 1 Peter 2. 2–10 : John 14. 1–14

Lord, guide us that we may walk in your way, rejoice in your truth,
and be kept for ever in the life which you give, which is eternal;
through him who lived and died and rose again for us,
Jesus Christ our Lord. **Amen.**

Lord, as you have called us to walk in your way,
make us the people that you would have us be,
guide us that we may do what you would have us do,
that we may reveal your truth, and lead others to the fullness of life,
that we may be a chosen people, a royal priesthood,
that we may proclaim the mighty acts of him who called us out of darkness into his marvellous light.
Lord, lead us in the ways of peace.
Guide us in the path of life.

We pray for all who are in positions of authority,
for all who will be called upon to make difficult decisions this week.
We remember those who make decisions that affect the life of this planet.
We pray for all who do research into healing and the renewal of the earth.
Lord, lead us in the ways of peace.
Guide us in the path of life.

We praise you for all who have enriched our lives,
for all who have built up our community,
for those who extended our vision,
for all who taught us the truth,
for those who set us on a good path.
We pray for our families and friends,
for the people we work with
   and those we spend our leisure-time with.
Lord, lead us in the ways of peace.
Guide us in the path of life.

We pray for all who are confused about the truth, or about life,
for all whose minds are disturbed,
for all who have lost their way.
We pray for all who live a lie and cannot face reality.
We pray for all who are not at peace.
We come to you with all who are troubled in heart.
Lord, lead us in the ways of peace.
Guide us in the path of life.

Lord Christ, as you have gone before us
   and prepared a place for us,
lead us until we come fully
into your kingdom
and walk before you in that life which is eternal.
Lord, lead us in the ways of peace.
Guide us in the path of life.

THE PEACE

Jesus says, 'Do not let your heart be troubled; believe in God,
believe also in me.'
The peace of the Lord be always with you
and also with you.

The good and gracious God guide us into the ways that lead to peace; and the blessing...

The Sixth Sunday of Easter

Acts 17. 22–31 : Ps. 66. 8–20 : 1 Peter 3. 13–22 : John 14. 15–21

Lord Jesus, you have promised to be with us for ever;
teach us to rejoice in your presence,
free us from all anxiety,
help us to know you are always at hand,
that we may work with you and to your glory,
Jesus our Lord, who with the Father and the Holy Spirit
lives and reigns for ever. **Amen**.

Lord, in you we live and move and have our being,
for we are your children,
    and you are not far from any one of us.
We pray for all who are being prepared for baptism or
    confirmation,
and that we with them may know that we dwell in you and you
    in us.
We pray for Christians who are struggling in lonely or difficult
    places,
for all who feel forsaken,
for all who are longing to know your love.
We pray for all who seek to do your will
    and fulfil your commandments.

Lord, you abide in us.
May we know we abide in you.

We pray for countries where laws are being flouted.
We pray for nations and peoples who are in danger of
    destroying themselves or others.
We remember areas of civil strife,
    areas where people are misused or abused.
We pray for all who seek to live in simplicity,
    gentleness and reverence,
for all who suffer for doing good.
Lord, you abide in us.
May we know we abide in you.

By your indwelling presence make our hearts and our homes
    places of peace.
We pray for peace in our communities,
for peace in our relationships,
that your peace may spread throughout our world.
Lord, you abide in us.
May we know we abide in you.

We pray for all who are captives to superstition or ignorance,
for all who have no knowledge of God,
for all whose lives are empty, or filled with the wrong things.
We remember before you all whose lives are falling apart,
all who are entering into darkness or sickness,
that each in their weakness may know your strength.
Lord, you abide in us.
May we know we abide in you.

Lord if we abide in you and you are in us,
    we are already in the fullness of that life which is eternal.
We rejoice in your presence, and pray for loved ones and friends
    who have gone before us.
Lord, you abide in us.
May we know we abide in you.

Jesus said, 'Abide in me and I will abide in you.'
The peace of the Lord be always with you
and also with you.

THE BLESSING

Christ, the Lord of the living and the dead, who died and rose
to life eternal, grant that you may abide in him and belong to
him for ever; and the blessing...

Ascension Day

Acts 1. 1–11 *or* Daniel 7. 9–14 : Ps. 47 *or* Ps. 93 : Ephesians 1. 15–23
or Acts 1. 1–11 : Luke 24. 44–53

Risen and Ascended Lord,
you have promised to be with us always;
teach us to be aware of your presence,
and to abide in your love,
that we may walk in the way that leads to glory,
where you live and reign with the Father and the Holy Spirit,
one God, world without end. **Amen.**

Lord Jesus Christ, you came down to lift us up,
you descended that we may ascend;
grant us a glimpse of your glory.
Give to your church a vision of your presence
that it may proclaim your peace and your love.

We pray for all who have lost vision,
for those whose lives are clouded with doubt and fear.
We remember those whose lives have become dull.
May we all learn to walk in the joy of your presence.
King of kings and Lord of lords,
lift us up into your glory.

We long for the time when the kingdoms of the world
    become your kingdom.
We pray that the peace you offer may be accepted
    by rulers and leaders;
that all in authority may rule with gentleness but firmness.
We pray for all who are not at peace
    with themselves or with others.
We remember all who feel neglected and forsaken in our world.
We pray for the world poor,
for all who are in bad housing,
for all who live in squalor,
for all who feel the days are dark, and that the going is rough.
King of kings and Lord of lords,
lift us up into your glory.

We give thanks that you are with us always:
your presence transforms our homes and our relationships.
We bring before you the needs of our families and friends.
We pray for all who desire to improve our communities.
May those who seek to change our lives
    be people of vision.
King of kings and Lord of lords,
lift us up into your glory.

We come to you with all who are down at this time,
may they know the power of your ascension,
in you may they find new hope and new courage.
We pray for all who are seriously ill,
    especially . . . .
for those whose powers are waning,

for all who cannot cope on their own.
We remember those who have the care of them.
Give us all a vision of your saving power.
King of kings and Lord of lords,
lift us up into your glory.

We rejoice that you are our great high priest
    who has ascended into heaven,
and that there you make intercession for us.
Lord, we join our prayers with yours, and we pray that our
    loved ones departed may rejoice in your kingdom.
King of kings and Lord of lords,
lift us up into your glory.

THE PEACE

Know that the risen and ascended Lord promises to be with you
for ever; and the peace of the Lord be always with you
and also with you.

THE BLESSING

The risen and ascended Lord be with you to uplift you, to
inspire you, to guide you, to give you a glimpse of glory; and the
blessing...

The Seventh Sunday of Easter
(Sunday after Ascension Day)

Acts 1. 6–14 : Ps. 68. 1–10 [32–35] : 1 Peter 4. 12–14; 5. 6–11 : John 17. 1–11

Lord, as your Son has ascended, let us not be weighed down by sin, but look to him who has brought us everlasting glory, and now reigns with you and the Holy Spirit in your kingdom for ever. **Amen.**

Risen and ascended Lord, come among us.
Fill us with your glory.

Deliver your church from the evil one.
Destroy the works of darkness,
and help us to walk as children of the light,
that we may proclaim you as King of kings and Lord of lords.
Risen and ascended Lord, come among us.
Fill us with your glory.

Deliver your creation from corruption.
Free us from the powers of evil.
Bring us into the glorious liberty of the children of God,
that the kingdoms of the world may become the Kingdom of God.
Risen and ascended Lord, come among us.
Fill us with your glory.

Vanquish our emptiness and confusion.
Free us from hard-heartedness,

that our homes may be uplifted,
that our hearts may be raised.
Risen and ascended Lord, come among us.
Fill us with your glory.

That the despairing and discouraged may find hope,
that the downtrodden may rise to new freedoms,
that the downcast may be lifted up,
that the weak, the ill, the dying, may be given hope, courage
   and strength,
Risen and ascended Lord, come among us.
Fill us with your glory.

That all may, in heart and mind, ascend
   and experience your power and your glory,
that we may rejoice with our loved ones
   who are in the fullness of your kingdom.
Risen and ascended Lord, come among us.
Fill us with your glory.

THE PEACE

The Lord our God is a mighty king: rejoice and be glad and
praise him for his greatness.
The peace of the Lord be always with you
and also with you.

THE BLESSING

Rejoice this day, for Christ has ascended into heaven.
Christ has opened the gate of glory.
Christ ever prays for us at the right hand of the Father.
Christ descended to lift us up to be with him.
And the blessing . . .

Day of Pentecost

———

Acts 2. 1–21 *or* Numbers 11. 24–30 : Ps. 104. 24–34, 35b (*or* 24–36) :
1 Corinthians 12. 3b–13 *or* Acts 2. 1–21 : John 20. 19–23 *or* John 7. 37–39

Lord God Almighty, pour upon us your Spirit,
and set us on fire with love for you,
that we may bring forth the fruits of love, joy and peace,
and live to the praise of your holy name;
through Jesus Christ our Lord. **Amen.**

Come, Holy Spirit. Come,
renew the face of the earth.

Holy Spirit, bringing order out of chaos,
bring order to our actions and purpose to our lives.
Come,
renew the face of the earth.

Holy Spirit, moving in the deep places of creation,
move in the depth of our hearts.
Come,
renew the face of the earth.

Holy Spirit, breathing life into all creatures,
refresh, renew, restore your people.
Come,
renew the face of the earth.

Holy Spirit, giver of all good gifts,
help us to use our talents and abilities aright.

Come,
renew the face of the earth.

Holy Spirit, giving life to dry bones,
give hope and joy to all who are weary.
Restore the lives which without you are dead.
Come,
renew the face of the earth.

Holy Spirit, giver of love,
kindle the hearts which without you are dull and cold.
Fill your church, our hearts and minds with love.
Come,
renew the face of the earth.

Come, Holy Spirit, upon the newly baptized
    and all new Christians.
Come upon the recently confirmed
    and all who are growing in their faith.
Come upon all who are testing their vocations
    and all who are in new work.
Come upon all bishops, priests and deacons,
    upon all who seek to serve you.
Come upon all who strive to proclaim your power
    and your presence.
Come upon the powerless and the oppressed.
Come, be known among the unemployed
    and the exploited.
Come and comfort the anxious and the fearful.
Come and give strength to the ill and the dying.
Come, Holy Spirit. Come,
renew the face of the earth.

THE PEACE

Jesus said to them: 'Peace be with you. As the Father sends me,
so I send you.' When he had said this he breathed on them and
said to them, 'Receive the Holy Spirit.'
The peace of the Lord be always with you
and also with you.

THE BLESSING

The fire of God change you, and you shall be changed.
The wind of God change you, and you shall be changed.
The breath of God change you, and you shall be changed.
The Spirit of God change you, and you shall be changed.
And the blessing...

Ordinary Time

Trinity Sunday

———

Isaiah 40. 12–17, 27–31 : Ps. 8 : 2 Corinthians 13. 11–13 : Matthew 28. 16–20

Holy, holy, holy God;
Holy and Strong One,
Holy and Mighty One,
Holy and Immortal One,
Holy Three, Holy One,
Be with us now and evermore.
Be with us now and evermore. **Amen.**

Holy Father, you have created all things
   and made us in your own image.
We rejoice in the beauty of your creation.
We come before you in wonder and awe.
We seek to be sensitive to your mysteries.
We pray for places where your earth is exploited or marred,
where your creatures are abused or misused.
We pray for all who lack freedom or are oppressed.
Holy God, Holy and Strong one,
hear our prayer.

Christ in glory, risen and ascended,
You have redeemed us by your love,
you give us life which is eternal.
We pray to you for all who walk in darkness,

all who cry out in pain, all who feel beyond hope.
We remember all who are rejected
   and are outcasts in our world.
Holy God, Holy and Strong One,
hear our prayer.

Spirit of God, breathing life into all,
we give you thanks for our talents and abilities,
for the powers of renewal and refreshment.
We pray that we and all your church may reach out in love.
We pray for bishops, priests and deacons,
for the ministry of all your faithful people.
We pray for the outreach and mission of your church.
Holy God, Holy and Strong One,
hear our prayer.

Holy, blessed and glorious Trinity,
One in Three, Three in One,
Bind us together in unity.
Bind us together in love.
Bind us together with loved ones departed.
Bind us together with your saints in glory.
Holy God, Holy and Strong One,
hear our prayer.

THE PEACE

He gives power to the faint, and strengthens the powerless.
Those who wait upon the Lord shall renew their strength.
The peace of the Lord be always with you
and also with you.

THE BLESSING

The goodness of the Creator,
the grace of the Saviour,

and the guidance of the Holy Spirit,
be upon you and within you;
and the blessing...

Proper 4

Sunday between 29 May and 4 June inclusive (if after Trinity Sunday)

Track 1
Genesis 6. 9–22; 7. 24; 8. 14–19
Ps. 46
Romans 1. 16–17, 3. 22b–28 [29–31]
Matthew 7. 21–29

Track 2
Deuteronomy 11. 18–21, 26–28
Ps. 31. 1–5, 19–24
Romans 1. 16–17; 3. 22b–28 [29–31]
Matthew 7. 21–29

Lord God, you are our rock,
a very present help in trouble:
strengthen us to work to your glory,
that we may proclaim your love,
live in faith,
and build on the firm foundation of Christ our Lord,
who is alive and reigns with you and the Holy spirit,
one God, world without end. **Amen.**

O Lord our God, when we and your church are beset
  by change and by storms
may we stand firm on that sure foundation which is Christ our
  Lord.
May we not be turned aside into that which is less than the full
  gospel.
Protect all who seek to defend the faith.
Strengthen all who look for hope and guidance.

Support all who are in doubt or whose faith is wavering at this
  time.
Be our strong rock, O Lord.
Be to us a tower of strength.

We pray for all leaders of peoples,
all who influence the minds of others,
all those who are setting standards for our society,
that what they teach may be on a firm foundation.
We pray for all who seek to keep peace,
all who seek to keep law and order,
all involved in broadcasting, in radio, television and the press.
Be our strong rock, O Lord.
Be to us a tower of strength.

We remember with affection those who taught us the faith.
We pray for our homes and our loved ones,
  for our security and protection.
We pray for all places of learning, for schools, colleges and
  universities.
We pray for all who are leaders of the young.
Be our strong rock, O Lord.
Be to us a tower of strength.

We remember all whose lives have crumbled this week,
those who have lost home, loved ones or possessions.
We pray for those who have become unemployed.
We pray for all who have incurred debts
  and now cannot repay.
We remember all who have become ill this week,
all who have become dependent on others.
Be our strong rock, O Lord.
Be to us a tower of strength.

We pray for all who have passed through that great flood we
  call death;
in your power and in your love they rejoice in eternal life.

We pray especially for..............
Grant that with them we may one day rejoice in your kingdom.
Be our strong rock, O Lord.
Be to us a tower of strength.

THE PEACE

The Lord of hosts is with us, the God of Jacob is our stronghold.
The peace of the Lord be always with you
and also with you.

THE BLESSING

Be strong in the Lord and in the power of his might; and the
blessing...

Proper 5

Sunday between 5 and 11 June inclusive (if after Trinity Sunday)

Track 1
Genesis 12. 1–9
Ps. 33. 1–12
Romans 4. 13–25
Matthew 9. 9–13, 18–26

Track 2
Hosea 5.15—6.6
Ps. 50. 7–15
Romans 4. 13–25
Matthew 9. 9–13, 18–26

Lord, as you have called us,
make us worthy of our calling.
As we reach out to touch you,
touch us, and we shall be changed,

that we may live to your glory,
Jesus Christ our Lord. **Amen.**

Lord God, help us to trust in you,
that we may hope beyond hope and trust beyond trust.
Let people see the faith of your church.
Let us witness to your almighty power;
though our faith is small it is in a great God.
May we help to uplift your people,
to raise the fallen and bring the sick to recovery.
Lord, heal us
and raise us up.

Heal, O Lord, the wounds of our world.
We pray for all who suffer from hunger,
for the outcasts of our society.
We pray for those who are lepers, those who have AIDS.
We pray for communities devastated by storms, earthquakes or
    war.
Lord, heal us
and raise us up.

Lord, enter our homes
and bring healing and peace to any divisions,
that we may be one in you.
Show us the way that leads to life.
Teach us to forgive and to accept forgiveness.
Cure the minds that are full of resentment and darkness.
Lord, heal us
and raise us up.

We give thanks for the work of doctors and nurses.
We pray for all hospitals and places of healing,
for faith healers and bringers of peace.
We pray for friends and loved ones who are sick.
We remember those who have ill children,
    and children at the point of death.

We pray for those who have borne long with sickness, for which there seems no cure.
Lord, heal us
and raise us up.

We give thanks for all whom you have lifted up from death and raised to life eternal.
We rejoice with the saints who have triumphed over the troubles of this world,
and are where sorrow and pain are no more.
Lord, heal us
and raise us up.

THE PEACE

Above all virtues, put love. Let the peace of Christ rule in your hearts; and the peace of the Lord be always with you
and also with you.

THE BLESSING

The Lord hold you in the palm of his hand, and give you life which is eternal. And the blessing...

Proper 6

Sunday between 12 and 18 June inclusive (if after Trinity Sunday)

Track 1	Track 2
Genesis 18. 1–15 [21. 1–7]	Exodus 19. 2–8a
Ps. 116. 1–2, 12–19 (*or* 11–18)	Ps. 100
Romans 5. 1–8	Romans 5. 1–8
Matthew 9.35—10.8 [9–23]	Matthew 9.35—10.8 [9–23]

Lord, as you have called us, make us worthy of our calling.
Guide us, that we may become the people you would have us
  be.
Direct us, that we may do what you would have us do;
through Jesus Christ our Lord. **Amen.**

Lord, you are with us as we proclaim the good news,
as we reach out to heal, to cure, to raise up;
you are with us as we battle against evil.
We pray for the church throughout the world,
for all involved in mission and outreach.
Lord, as you call us,
make us worthy of our calling.

Lord, you have called us to work together.
We pray for the work of the United Nations.
We remember all who are seeking to build up communities.
We pray for those in government, and leaders of industries.
We pray for all who have a sense of vocation and dedication.
We remember those whose work is thwarted by the greed or
  violence of others.

Lord, as you call us,
make us worthy of our calling.

We give thanks for all who have called us to a knowledge of
    you.
We pray for those who have sacrificed for us,
those who love us, and those whom we love.
We give thanks for all who have been examples to us,
and pray that we may be an example to others.
Lord, as you call us,
make us worthy of our calling.

We give thanks for carers, for home helps and social workers.
We pray for all whose vocation is cut short by sickness or
    disease,
for all whose lives are restricted by poverty or oppression.
We pray for all who have lost any sense of vocation or meaning
    to life.
Lord, as you call us,
make us worthy of our calling.

We are glad for all who have fulfilled their calling
    and have entered the fullness of your kingdom.
We pray that, like them, we may follow you for ever.
Lord, as you call us,
make us worthy of our calling.

THE PEACE

Since we are justified by faith, we have peace with God through
our Lord Jesus Christ.
The peace of the Lord be always with you
and also with you.

The love of God has been poured into our hearts through the Holy Spirit he has given us; and the blessing...

Proper 7

Sunday between 19 and 25 June inclusive (if after Trinity Sunday)

———

Track 1
Genesis 21. 8–21
Ps. 86. 1–10 [16–17]
Romans 6. 1b–11
Matthew 10. 24–39

Track 2
Jeremiah 20. 7–13
Ps. 69. 7–10 [11–15] 16–18
Romans 6. 1b–11
Matthew 10. 24–39

Lord Jesus Christ, everlasting Son of the Father, who for our sakes humbled yourself, help us to heed your call. Give us a spirit of humble service that we may reach out to others in love, Christ our Lord, who with the Father and the Spirit lives and reigns for evermore. **Amen.**

Lord, you have called us to serve you,
you have called us to heal,
you have called us to love.
Bless the work of the church in places of neglect and
    deprivation.
We pray for all who work in the healing ministry.
Lord, we come to you,
for you alone can make us whole.

We pray for all who work in the world of commerce,
for bankers, tax-collectors, insurance brokers.
We remember all who are deeply in debt and cannot repay.
We pray for countries where the national debt is crippling.
Lord, we come to you,
for you alone can make us whole.

Lord, may we come reaching out to touch you;
may we come in faith.
We pray for those who brought us to your presence.
We pray for homes where there is chronic illness,
 or the illness of a child.
Lord, we come to you,
for you alone can make us whole.

We remember before you all who are outcasts.
We pray for the broken-hearted and the broken-spirited.
We pray for all who find themselves in desperate situations.
For all who are anxious about their health or the health of a
 loved one.
Lord, we come to you,
for you alone can make us whole.

We give thanks for all who have been restored by your touch,
and all whom you have raised from the point of death.
We pray especially for . . . .
Lord, we come to you,
for you alone can make us whole.

THE PEACE

Know that Christ, being raised from the dead, will never die
again; and the peace of the Lord be always with you
and also with you.

Consider yourself dead to sin and alive to God in Christ Jesus; and the blessing...

Proper 8

Sunday between 26 June and 2 July inclusive

———

Track 1	Track 2
Genesis 22. 1–14	Jeremiah 28. 5–9
Ps. 13	Ps. 89. 1–4, 15–18 (*or* 8–18)
Romans 6. 12–23	Romans 6. 12–23
Matthew 10. 40–42	Matthew 10. 40–42

Lord, you have freed us from the slavery of sin,
and called us to be sons and daughters of God.
Help us to work for the freedom of all who are captives,
and for the bringing in of your kingdom, Jesus Christ our Lord,
who reigns with the Father and the Holy Spirit
for ever and ever. **Amen.**

We pray for your church,
that it may be a holy church, a serving church.
May we reveal your love through our care for and our
    acceptance of others.
We pray for the work of the church among the poor and the
    oppressed,
that in you we may come to the glorious liberty of the children
    of God.

Amen,
may the Lord do it.

Guide the leaders of nations and communities into the way of
  peace and good will.
We pray for those who strive to bring peace between various
  factions,
for all who seek to bring unity and harmony to our world,
that they may all be guided by your Spirit.
Amen,
may the Lord do it.

Lord, make our homes places of holiness and hospitality.
In our dealings fill us with grace and goodness,
make us welcoming and friendly.
Amen,
may the Lord do it.

We remember before you all prisoners of conscience,
all who are in prison through injustice and tyranny.
We pray for the work of Amnesty International.
We pray for all who have lost their freedom
  through sickness and immobility.
We pray for the world-weary, the heavily burdened,
  the worn out and the broken,
that all may know in their hearts the glorious liberty of the
  children of God.
Amen,
may the Lord do it.

We give thanks for all who are now victorious,
all who have left behind the restrictions of this life
  and are walking before you as children of God.
We pray especially for . . . .
May we, with them, know your abiding presence.
Amen,
may the Lord do it.

THE PEACE

The gift of God is eternal life in Christ Jesus our Lord.
The peace of the Lord be always with you
and also with you.

THE BLESSING

The good and gracious Lord grant you to know the glorious
liberty of the children of God; and the blessing...

Proper 9

Sunday between 3 and 9 July inclusive

———

Track 1
Genesis 24. 34–38, 42–49, 58–67
Ps. 45. 10–17
or Canticle: Song of Sol. 2. 8–13
Romans 7. 15–25a
Matthew 11. 16–19, 25–30

Track 2
Zechariah 9. 9–12
Ps. 145. 8–14
Romans 7. 15–25a
Matthew 11. 16–19, 25–30

Come, Lord, come to us, that we may find rest and peace in
 you.
Come, Lord, come to us, that we may love you and proclaim
 your saving power,
that we may live to your glory, Jesus Christ,
who with the Father and the Holy Spirit is worshipped
for ever and ever. **Amen.**

We give thanks to you for all who labour for the coming in of
    your kingdom.
We pray for visionaries, preachers, pastors, evangelists and
    carers,
We pray for those who are dispirited by the greatness of the
    task facing them,
for all who are wearied by their work,
for those without human support,
for all who work in lonely and dangerous places.
We come with our tiredness and our weariness.
Lord, we come to you.
Give us rest and refreshment.

We pray for all who have lost the joy and pleasure of living,
for the bored, the cynical, and all who are jaded with life.
We remember all who are overworked and stressed.
We pray for all who cannot relax and enjoy being themselves.
Lord, we come to you.
Give us rest and refreshment.

Lord, make our homes places of peace and calm.
We pray for families where there is strife,
for relationships that are at the point of breaking.
We pray for those whose lives have become dull.
Lord, we come to you.
Give us rest and refreshment.

We pray for all who are over-anxious,
for the depressed and the despairing,
for all who are suffering from a breakdown.
We pray for all who are no longer coping on their own.
We come with our own burdens and needs.
Lord, we come to you.
Give us rest and refreshment.

We give thanks for those who are at rest
    and have found newness of life in you.

We pray for all whose suffering is over
  and are restored and renewed in your kingdom.
We pray especially for . . . .
We pray that with them we may know your almighty power.
Lord, we come to you.
Give us rest and refreshment.

THE PEACE

The Lord upholds all those who fall. He lifts up those who are
  bowed down.
The peace of the Lord be always with you
and also with you.

THE BLESSING

The good and gracious God grant you refreshment, renewal,
restoration, that in his power you may live and work to his
glory; and the blessing . . .

Proper 10

Sunday between 10 and 16 July inclusive

Track 1
Genesis 25. 19–34
Ps. 119. 105–112
Romans 8. 1–11
Matthew 13. 1–9, 18–23

Track 2
Isaiah 55. 10–13
Ps. 65. [1–8] 9–13
Romans 8. 1–11
Matthew 13. 1–9, 18–23

Lord of the harvest, make us fruitful in good works.
Help us to share in your salvation,
   and enjoy bringing in your harvest;
through Jesus Christ our Lord. **Amen.**

We pray for all evangelists, preachers and pastors.
We pray for those who teach in Sunday schools and Bible
   groups.
We remember all who go out to seek and save the lost.
We are sorry for times when we stray away from you,
when we are tempted to lose hope.
God, you are our salvation.
You are the hope of us all.

We pray for all who have unrewarding work to do,
for all whose cries fall on stony ground,
for all who labour but whose fulfilment is frustrated,
for all who are choked by the cares and the riches of the world.
We remember all who have lost hope of growing or achieving
   anything.

God, you are our salvation.
You are the hope of us all.

Help us to bring forth the fruits of your Spirit in our homes.
May our homes be places where love, joy and peace abound.
May we nurture the young in the ways of truth and goodness.
We pray for the homeless,
for those who look in hope to have a home of their own.
God, you are our salvation.
You are the hope of us all.

Lord, have mercy on all who have lost hope or vision.
Protect all who are not at peace in themselves
 or at peace with those around them.
We pray for all who are in sickness or adversity,
for all who are tempted to give up,
for all who are suffering from a breakdown,
 or unable to cope on their own.
We pray for friends and loved ones in sickness,
 especially . . . .
Lord, set our minds on the Spirit, on life and peace.
God, you are our salvation.
You are the hope of us all.

We give thanks that as you raised Christ from the dead you will
 give life to our mortal bodies.
We pray for all who are renewed and refreshed in your eternal
 kingdom,
and pray that one day we may share with them in that glory.
God you are our salvation.
You are the hope of us all.

God is our salvation and the hope of all the ends of the earth.
The peace of the Lord be always with you
and also with you.

The God of grace, who has called you to his eternal glory in
Christ Jesus our Lord, restore, establish, strengthen you in all
goodness; and the blessing...

Proper 11

Sunday between 17 and 23 July inclusive

Track 1	Track 2
Genesis 28. 10–19a	Wisdom of Solomon 12. 13, 16–19 *or*
Ps. 139. 1–12 [23–24]	Isaiah 44. 6–8
Romans 8. 12–25	Ps. 86. 11–17
Matthew 13. 24–30, 36–43	Romans 8. 12–25
	Matthew 13. 24–30, 36–43

O God, be a tower of strength to all who trust in you; and
because through the weakness of our mortal nature we can do
no good without you, empower us to work for your freedom
and peace; through Jesus Christ our Lord. **Amen.**

With all your church we pray for all who are longing and
  yearning for freedom.
Lord, look in mercy on all who are struggling in life.

Strengthen all who are being persecuted for their faith.
Guide us as we seek to grow in our faith,
that we may be led by the Spirit to become children of God.
Good and gracious God,
grant us a glimpse of your glory.

We pray for all who are caught up in corruption and decay.
Forgive us where we destroy and mar your world through
     greed.
We pray for areas where forests are being destroyed, the soil
     eroded, the water polluted.
Guide by your Spirit all who groan for a better world,
all who seek to restore and renew the earth.
Good and gracious God,
grant us a glimpse of your glory.

We come with our own inner longings and hopes,
that your glory may be revealed in our homes
     and in our lives,
that we may know that we are all children of God
     and treat each other with respect.
We pray for all who live in poor or slum housing,
for those who have no home.
Good and gracious God,
grant us a glimpse of your glory.

Lord, look in mercy on all who find life futile,
all who are bored, all whose work is unrewarding or dull,
all who feel they have wasted their lives,
all who are surrounded by decay and decadence.
We pray for all who are struggling through sickness or
     disability,
all who are wearied by caring for others.
May they know that the sufferings of this present time are
     nothing to be compared with the glory that shall be revealed
     in us.

Good and gracious God,
grant us a glimpse of your glory.

We rejoice in your salvation,
that you call us to be sons and daughters of God,
that you call us out of death into life which is eternal.
We pray for our loved ones departed,
    especially ....
and for a vision of your glorious kingdom.
Good and gracious God,
grant us a glimpse of your glory.

THE PEACE

All who are led by the Spirit of God are children of God.
The peace of the Lord be always with you
and also with you.

THE BLESSING

The glory of God the Creator be yours,
the glory of Christ the Redeemer be yours,
the glory of the Spirit, the Sanctifier be yours;
and the blessing...

Proper 12

Sunday between 24 and 30 July inclusive

———

Track 1
Genesis 29. 15–28
Ps. 105. 1–11 [45b]
or Ps. 128
Romans 8. 26–39
Matthew 13. 31–33, 44–52

Track 2
1 Kings 3. 5–12
Ps. 119. 129–136
Romans 8. 26–39
Matthew 13. 31–33, 44–52

Spirit, in our weakness be our strength.
We do not know how to pray as we ought.
As we love you, work in us that which is good;
through Jesus Christ our Lord. **Amen**.

Lord, as you have called us to fulfil your purpose,
work in us and through us to do your will.
Make us the people you want us to be.
Guide us to do what you would have us do.
We pray for all who are seeking to grow in the faith,
for all seekers, and enquirers.
Lord, your will be done,
your kingdom come in us.

We pray for all who are suffering hardship or persecution,
for all who are in peril or danger.
Strengthen all who seek to bring in your kingdom
    by striving for peace, for justice, for liberty.
May we be conquerors of darkness and evil
    through him who loves us.

Lord, your will be done,
your kingdom come in us.

We give thanks for those who have shared with us
   the riches of the kingdom,
for those who have been examples to us,
for those who have taught us the faith.
We pray for all who seek to pass on these riches
   in their homes and in the community.
Lord, your will be done,
your kingdom come in us.

Lord, have mercy on all who are suffering persecution, peril or
   the sword.
May they know your love and your saving power.
We remember people who are suffering through tyranny and
   violence.
We pray for all who have been injured through accidents,
For all who have fallen into sickness or disability,
for those losing agility or mobility,
for all healers and comforters.
Lord, your will be done,
your kingdom come in us.

We give thanks that in Christ we are more than conquerors.
In him you have brought us to the great riches of the kingdom.
We pray for the saints and the faithful departed,
especially for . . . .
that we may all be one with you in your eternal kingdom.
Lord, your will be done,
your kingdom come in us.

THE PEACE

Nothing shall separate us from the love of God in Christ Jesus
   our Lord.
The peace of the Lord be always with you
and also with you.

THE BLESSING

The love of God enfold you,
the power of Christ protect you,
the leading of the Spirit guide you;
and the blessing . . .

Proper 13

Sunday between 31 July and 6 August inclusive

———

Track 1	*Track 2*
Genesis 32. 22–31	Isaiah 55. 1–5
Ps. 17. 1–7 (15)	Ps. 145. [8–9] 14–21
Romans 9. 1–5	Romans 9. 1–5
Matthew 14. 13–21	Matthew 14. 13–21

Lord, you are the bread of heaven, giving life to the world.
You fill our emptiness with your goodness.
You come to our weakness with your strength.
Come, refresh, renew, restore us,
Jesus Christ our Lord,

who with the Father and the Holy Spirit
lives in glory everlasting. **Amen.**

We pray that your church may hunger and thirst after
    righteousness.
May your church seek to care for and feed the hungry in spirit.
May we seek out the lost, and those in desert places,
and offer them the sustenance of the gospel.
We pray for Bible study groups and outreach groups.
Lord, you are the bread of life.
Feed us now and evermore.

We remember before you the starving peoples of our world,
those who suffer from famine, poverty or war,
all whose lives are diminished through malnutrition and
    neglect.
Let the harvests of our world be neither hoarded nor
    squandered.
We pray for all whose lives are fragmented,
for all who are broken.
Lord, you open your hands and satisfy the needs of every
    creature.
Lord, you are the bread of life.
Feed us now and evermore.

We give thanks for those who have fed us and cared for us.
We remember all who have shown compassion and tenderness.
Lord, bless our loved ones, our homes and our communities.
Fill our deep longing for you with your presence and your
    peace.
Lord, you are the bread of life.
Feed us now and evermore.

We pray for all who feel drained and empty,
all who have no energy or strength.
Lord, have compassion upon the weak, the weary,
the harassed and the helpless.

We come to you for renewal, refreshment and hope.
Lord, you are the bread of life.
Feed us now and evermore.

We give thanks for those who no longer hunger or thirst for
    they have been refreshed in your kingdom.
May we look forward to the day when we share with them in
    the glory which is everlasting.
Lord, you are the bread of life.
Feed us now and evermore.

THE PEACE

Peace and mercy to the people of God.
The peace of the Lord be always with you
and also with you.

THE BLESSING

The love of Jesus sustain you,
the joy of Jesus fill you,
the power of Jesus strengthen you;
and the blessing...

Proper 14

Sunday between 7 and 13 August inclusive

Track 1
Genesis 37. 1–4, 12–28
Ps. 105. 1–6, 16–22, 45b
(*or* vv1–10)
Romans 10. 5–15
Matthew 14. 22–33

Track 2
1 Kings 19. 9–18
Ps. 85. 8–13
Romans 10. 5–15
Matthew 14. 22–33

Lord, in the storms of life, bid us come to you,
that we, who are aware of our weakness,
may be made strong;
through the power of Christ our Lord. **Amen.**

When we are in danger of being overwhelmed,
   increase our faith.
When troubles beset us, let us hear you say,
   'Take heart, it is I: do not be afraid.'
Give to your church a new vision of yourself and of your saving
   power.
Go with us as we go out to proclaim your love.
We pray for areas where the church is struggling
   or being overwhelmed,
for all evangelists and pastors who are overworked or in
   danger.
We pray for all who reach out in faith towards you.
Show us your mercy, O Lord,
and grant us your salvation.

We pray for areas of the world where there have been floods or
    other natural disasters,
for all who are swamped by poverty or hunger,
for all who are battered by wave after wave of oppression or
    violence,
for those who have no freedom,
for all who are sinking beneath a load of care and anxiety.
Show us your mercy, O Lord,
and grant us your salvation.

We give thanks for all who have supported us
    in times of trouble or distress.
We pray for friends who are in need at this time.
We pray that we will not be a burden to any, but a strength.
We remember all who are finding caring for their home
    overwhelming.
Show us your mercy, O Lord,
and grant us your salvation.

We pray for all who are down,
the fearful, the weary, the despairing.
We pray for all who are unable to help themselves.
We remember all who give a helping hand.
We pray for carers, home helps, social workers.
We remember those who are suffering in their care of another.
Show us your mercy, O Lord,
and grant us your salvation.

We give thanks for those who are beyond the storms of this
    world
and have come to the haven of rest.
Though our faith is weak, we reach out to you,
for you are almighty.
Grant that we may come to be with your saints in life eternal.
Show us your mercy, O Lord,
and grant us your salvation.

THE PEACE

The Lord shall keep in perfect peace the minds that are fixed on
him.
The peace of the Lord be always with you
and also with you.

THE BLESSING

The Lord keep you safe in his grasp;
know that you can never fall out of the everlasting arms.
The Lord deliver you from all evil;
and the blessing...

Proper 15

Sunday between 14 and 20 August inclusive

———

Track 1
Genesis 45. 1–15
Ps. 133
Romans 11. 1–2a, 29–32
Matthew 15. [10–20] 21–28

Track 2
Isaiah 56. 1, 6–8
Ps. 67
Romans 11. 1–2a, 29–32
Matthew 15. [10–20] 21–28

Holy Father, grant us pardon and peace,
cleanse us from all sin,
confirm and strengthen us in all goodness,
and keep us in peace and life eternal;
through Jesus Christ our Lord. **Amen.**

Bless, O Lord, your church with the grace to proclaim your
    saving power,
that we may lead people from the captivity of fear and darkness
    into your light.
Forgive us our sins and divisions,
lead us to a new unity and harmony.
We pray for all who lead others to you through writing, art or
    music.
We pray for the hard-hearted and the insensitive.
Lord, help us.
Lord, have mercy upon us.

Forgive, O Lord, the sins that divide us.
We pray that artificial barriers between peoples or nations may
    come down.
We pray for ethnic minority groups,
for all who are judged because of their race, colour or creed.
We remember at this time all refugees, all outcasts and rejected
    peoples.
Lord, help us.
Lord, have mercy upon us.

We give you thanks for those who in love brought us to you,
for those who shared their faith and their love with us.
We pray for our homes and our loved ones.
We pray for homes where there is no faith,
    or where there is no love.
Lord, help us.
Lord, have mercy upon us.

We remember all who have loved ones in sickness.
We pray for children who are distressed or in pain.
Give courage and hope to all parents who are anxious for their
    children.
We pray for the disturbed;
we remember especially the autistic, and the schizophrenic.

We pray for all who are diminished by evil, sickness, or their
   surroundings.
Lord, help us.
Lord, have mercy upon us.

We remember all who have suffered a painful or violent death,
all who have died suddenly through accident or crime.
We pray that they may have a new freedom in your love.
Lord, help us.
Lord, have mercy upon us.

THE PEACE

Grace to you, forgiveness and peace through Christ the Saviour;
and the peace of the Lord be always with you
and also with you.

THE BLESSING

The God of grace and glory, restore, strengthen, guide you; and
the blessing . . .

Proper 16

Sunday between 21 and 27 August inclusive

———

Track 1
Exodus 1.8—2.10
Ps. 124
Romans 12. 1–8
Matthew 16. 13–20

Track 2
Isaiah 51. 1–6
Ps. 138
Romans 12. 1–8
Matthew 16. 13–20

Lord, transform us by your love,
that we may know and do your will,
that we may live and work to your praise and glory,
through Christ, the King of glory,
who lives and reigns with you and the Holy Spirit,
one God, world without end. **Amen.**

Lord we present ourselves, our souls and bodies, to you.
You give us life, you give us love, you give us yourself.
May we give our lives, our love, ourselves to you.
We pray for the unity of your church,
that we may work together for the good of all.
We give thanks for the gifts you have given to us;
let us use them to your glory.
We pray especially for all who exercise the gifts of ministry,
    teaching, and healing.
Christ, Son of the living God,
hear us and help us.

We pray for all people, that their talents and abilities may be
 able to be used.
Bless each in their vocation and work.
We remember those who have been made redundant, and the
 unemployed.
We pray for those whose work is dull and mechanical.
We remember all whose talents are wasted and thwarted.
Christ, Son of the living God,
hear us and help us.

Bless our homes with holiness and hospitality,
with cheerfulness and kindliness,
with generosity and with goodness.
We pray for our loved ones, our neighbours and our friends,
the communities to which we belong and the places where we
 work.
Christ, Son of the living God,
hear us and help us.

We pray for all who suffer through the cruelty of others,
for all who have no confidence in themselves or in the world.
We pray for all who find making relationships difficult.
We remember the lonely,
and those who have been rejected or betrayed.
We pray for all who are in trouble, need, sickness or any other
 adversity.
Christ, Son of the living God,
hear us and help us.

We give thanks for all who have been strengthened by their
 faith,
for all who have died in faith.
We give thanks for .... and pray for..............
Lord, grant us with them a share in your heavenly kingdom.
Christ, Son of the living God,
hear us and help us.

THE PEACE

Live in peace, pray for peace, act in peace; and the peace of the
Lord be always with you
and also with you.

THE BLESSING

The glory of the Father,
the peace of the Saviour,
the power of the Spirit,
be within you and about you;
and the blessing...

Proper 17

Sunday between 28 August and 3 September inclusive

———

Track 1
Exodus 3. 1–15
Ps. 105. 1–6, 23–26, 45b
(*or* Ps. 115)
Romans 12. 9–21
Matthew 16. 21–28

Track 2
Jeremiah 15. 15–21
Ps. 26. 1–8
Romans 12. 9–21
Matthew 16. 21–28

Lord, as you love us, help us to love one another.
Give to your church a burning zeal
    and keep us ardent in our spirits.
May we ever rejoice in the hope that you have set before us;
through Christ our living Lord. **Amen.**

Lord, we pray for unity and peace in your church.
Increase our fellowship with one another
    and our openness to others.
Give us the courage to proclaim the saving power of the cross.
May your church help to bring reconciliation and peace in your
    world.
Lord of glory,
grant us your peace.

We pray for peace in our hearts,
for peace in our communities,
for peace in your world,
that as much as is possible we may live at peace with all people.
We pray for peace-keeping forces, for the United Nations.
We pray for the police and probation services.
We give thanks for all peacemakers.
We pray for all who offer your peace to this world.
Lord of glory,
grant us your peace.

May our homes be places of peace and love,
homes of holiness and hospitality,
homes of harmony and of unity.
May we learn acceptance, and forgiveness, through our loved
    ones.
Let us not be overcome by evil, but overcome evil with good.
Lord of glory,
grant us your peace.

We pray for all who are not at peace,
for people of broken homes and broken relationships.
We pray for the broken-hearted and the broken in spirit,
for places where there is a breakdown of peace or wellbeing,
for all who are being destroyed by hatred or revenge,
remembering all who have suffered from the violence of others.
Lord of glory,
grant us your peace.

Lord, when you come in your glory,
make us to be one with you and the saints who are now at
  peace.
Lord of glory,
grant us your peace.

THE PEACE

If it is possible, so far as it depends on you, live peaceably with
all; and the peace of the Lord be always with you
and also with you.

THE BLESSING

The peace of God which passes all understanding,
the peace which the world cannot give,
be in your hearts and minds,
in your home and in your community;
and the blessing...

Proper 18

Sunday between 4 and 10 September inclusive

———

Track 1
Exodus 12. 1–14
Ps. 149
Romans 13. 8–14
Matthew 18. 15–20

Track 2
Ezekiel 33. 7–11
Ps. 119. 33–40
Romans 13. 8–14
Matthew 18. 15–20

Lord, awaken us to your glory.
Open our eyes to your presence.
Open our ears to your call.
Open our hearts to your love,
that we may proclaim that you are among us;
through Jesus Christ our Lord. **Amen**.

We pray for all who are seeking to set standards, to raise
     morale,
for all who are seeking holiness and dedication,
for all who are living heroic lives,
for all striving to live simply.
May we be a listening church and a forgiving church.
Lord, in your mercy
hear us and help us.

We pray for all who have lost sight of spiritual values,
all who are caught up in sheer materialism,
all who can measure only by possessions or wealth.
We pray for all who suffer from hunger, poverty or bad
     housing.

We pray for all who are caught up in debauchery and
   licentiousness.
Lord, in your mercy
hear us and help us.

We pray that our homes may reflect your acceptance and love.
Forgive our quarrelling and our jealousy.
Teach us tolerance and compassion.
We give thanks for all who have tolerated us,
   and given us their love.
We pray that our community may be a caring and friendly
   community.
Lord, in your mercy
hear us and help us.

We pray for all involved in drunkenness or vice,
all who are alcoholics or addicts.
We pray for homes that suffer through the sin or weakness of a
   member of the family,
for all who are subjected to violence or abuse.
We remember all who are tempted to give up hope.
Lord, in your mercy
hear us and help us.

We give thanks for all who have walked the way of your
   commandments,
who have fulfilled your laws and done your will.
Following their example, may we come to share with them in
   your everlasting glory.
Lord, in your mercy
hear us and help us.

THE PEACE

Become an instrument of God's peace; and the peace of the Lord be always with you
and also with you.

THE BLESSING

God's light guide you,
God's hand support you,
God's love surround you;
and the blessing...

Proper 19

Sunday between 11 and 17 September inclusive

Track 1
Exodus 14. 19–31
Ps. 114 *or Canticle:*
Exod. 15. 1b–11, 20–21
Romans 14. 1–12
Matthew 18. 21–35

Track 2
Genesis 50. 15–21
Ps. 103. [1–7] 8–13
Romans 14. 1–12
Matthew 18. 21–35

Lord, you opened your arms for us on the cross,
you welcome us into your kingdom:
may your saving power be known among us,
and lead us into the ways of peace,
Christ our Lord,
who lives and reigns with the Father and the Holy Spirit in
  everlasting love. **Amen.**

Lord, we pray that your church may be welcoming and open.
Let us draw others to you by our love and understanding.
May we be a support to the weak in faith,
    a strength to the wavering, and uplift the fallen.
Let us not be judgemental, and yet let us stand firm in our love
    for you and for your will.
Teach us to be forgiving towards others
    as we seek forgiveness from you.
We pray for the outreach of your church,
for its mission to seek out the lost and recover the fallen.
Lord, as you gave your life for us,
help us to give our lives to you.

We pray for the banks and commerce of our world.
We pray for countries and peoples that are deeply in debt.
We pray for justice and fair dealings in trade.
We remember those who have had homes or land repossessed,
all who have become bankrupt,
all who have lost the little that they had.
Lord, as you gave your life for us,
help us to give our lives to you.

We give thanks for what you have given to us.
We pray that what we have may be neither hoarded nor
    squandered,
that we may give to the relief of the needy
    and to the building up of our world.
We give thanks for all who have been generous to us,
and pray that our homes may be places of grace and generosity.
Lord, as you gave your life for us,
help us to give our lives to you.

We pray for those whose lives are diminished
    by greed and selfishness,
for all who are afraid to venture or to risk.
We remember those afraid to commit themselves,
all who have been hurt in love or betrayed by loved ones.

We pray for all whose relationships have broken down.
We remember before you all who are in trouble or in need.
We pray for those in sickness.
Lord, as you gave your life for us,
help us to give our lives to you.

We give thanks for all who in their generosity
   have given their lives in the service of others.
We pray that as they gave their love and their life,
   you will give them love and life eternal.
We pray especially for . . . .
May we, with them, share in your love
and in life everlasting.
Lord, as you gave your life for us,
help us to give our lives to you.

THE PEACE

Follow the things that make for peace; and the peace of the
Lord be always with you
and also with you.

THE BLESSING

The power of God be about you,
the love of Christ enfold you,
the joy of the Spirit be within you;
and the blessing . . .

Proper 20

Sunday between 18 and 24 September inclusive

Track 1	Track 2
Exodus 16. 2–15	Jonah 3.10—4.11
Ps. 105. [1–6] 37–45	Ps. 145. 1–8
Philippians 1. 21–30	Philippians 1. 21–30
Matthew 20. 1–16	Matthew 20. 1–16

Lord, teach us to live in a manner worthy of the gospel of
    Christ.
Let us not be intimidated by opposition or criticism.
Keep us firm in the faith you have set before us;
through Christ who has triumphed
and reigns with you and the Holy Spirit
for ever and ever. **Amen.**

We pray for Christians in areas where they are oppressed,
for those who face cynicism at home or at work,
for all who are afraid to confess their faith.
We remember those seeking to spread the gospel in non-
    Christian areas.
Lord, in your mercy
help us to be gracious to us.

Bless all employers with a spirit of fairness and grace.
We remember all who have to queue for work,
all who depend on Social Security.
We pray for all who are without work,
for those on low incomes,

for those who cannot get work through prejudice or protection
  rackets.
May all who prosper be generous and willing to share with the
  needy.
We pray for all relief organizations.
Lord, in your mercy
help us and be gracious to us.

We give thanks for our own work and our homes.
We pray for all who supply us with the things we need.
We remember homes where families go hungry,
those who are in great debt,
those who have had their homes repossessed.
Lord, in your mercy
help us and be gracious to us.

We remember all who are unable to work through disability.
We pray for all who are handicapped,
for all who are permanently on sickness benefit,
for the chronically ill,
for those who cannot do paid work for looking after a loved
  one who is ill.
Lord, in your mercy
help us and be gracious to us.

We give thanks for all who have been faithful labourers in your
  harvest;
may we with them rejoice in your love and generosity in your
  everlasting kingdom.
Lord, in your mercy
help us and be gracious to us.

THE PEACE

The dayspring from on high has dawned upon us, to give light
to those who dwell in darkness and to guide our feet into the

way of peace.
The peace of the Lord be always with you
and also with you.

THE BLESSING

The peace of God go with you wherever you travel,
the power of God protect you in every journey,
the spirit of God strengthen you for every task;
and the blessing...

Proper 21

Sunday between 25 September and 1 October inclusive

Track 1
Exodus 17. 1–7
Ps. 78. 1–4, 12–16 (*or* 1–7)
Philippians 2. 1–13
Matthew 21. 23–32

Track 2
Ezekiel 18. 1–4, 25–32
Ps. 25. 1–9
Philippians 2. 1–13
Matthew 21. 23–32

Lord, as you came down to lift us up,
help us to show compassion and sympathy to others.
Give to your church a sense of service and humility.
May we be obedient to you,
seeking to do your will at all times,
Jesus Christ our Lord. **Amen.**

As you have called us to know you,
you have called us to love you.
Lord, sustain us by your love

and make us worthy of our calling.
We pray for the church as it works in poor and difficult areas,
for the work of the church among outcasts and rejected people.
Lord, by your love
lead us and transform us.

We pray for the kingdoms of the world,
that they may become the kingdom of our God.
We pray that leaders of people and rulers may govern with
humility,
that they may not be full of selfish ambition or conceit,
that they may seek truly to serve and to meet the needs of their
people.
We pray for all who are exploited,
for all who are treated like slaves,
for all who yearn for freedom and justice.
Lord, by your love
lead us and transform us.

We give thanks for all who have given themselves for us in love,
for the sacrifice of parents and friends.
We pray that we may be generous towards all.
As we have richly received, may we richly give.
Teach us to be accepting and hospitable.
Lord, by your love
lead us and transform us.

Lord, bless all who find life difficult at this time.
We pray for those who have hard decisions to make this week.
We remember those who are having a hard time at home or at
work,
all who are suffering humiliation or degradation.
We pray for all who are brought low by sickness.
We remember especially . . . .
Lord, by your love
lead us and transform us.

We give thanks for all who have revealed the working of God in
   their lives and are now in glory.
We give thanks for saints and martyrs,
for all who have enriched the world by their willingness to
   sacrifice.
We pray that we may rejoice with them in your kingdom.
Lord, by your love
lead us and transform us.

THE PEACE

The deep peace of God be in your hearts and minds, in your
actions and in your life, and the peace of God be always with
you
and also with you.

THE BLESSING

Trust in him who raises the dead, and gives new life to our
mortal bodies: place all your hope on him; and the blessing...

Proper 22

Sunday between 2 and 8 October inclusive

Track 1
Exodus 20. 1–4, 7–9, 12–20
Ps. 19. [1–6] 7–14
Philippians 3. 4b–14
Matthew 21. 33–46

Track 2
Isaiah 5. 1–7
Ps. 80. 7–15
Philippians 3. 4b–14
Matthew 21. 33–46

Lord, you have called us to know you,
you have called us to love you,
you have called us to serve you.
Make us worthy of our calling.
May we proclaim your power and your peace.
May we rejoice in your light and in your love;
through Christ the living Lord. **Amen.**

We pray for the church that is under persecution,
the church at work in dangerous and dark places.
We pray for churches that have lost their vision;
for all who seek to bring the light of Christ to others,
that we all may grow in holiness and in outreach.
That we may know Christ
and the power of his resurrection.

We pray for all who are struggling for survival.
We pray for those whose lives have collapsed around them.
We remember those who have lost loved ones, possessions,
    homes or work this week,
all who have been robbed or stripped of their dignity,

those sleeping on the streets of our cities,
all who have lost hope or will-power.
That we may know Christ
and the power of his resurrection.

We pray that our homes may be places of peace and light,
that our relationships may reflect joy and love,
that our faith may fill our homes and our actions,
that we may work for peace and goodwill.
That we may know Christ
and the power of his resurrection.

We pray for all who are brought low by disease or sickness,
for those who have been taken into care this week,
for all who are terminally ill.
We pray for the hospice movement
and for all who care for the dying.
We remember all who have lost loved ones this week.
We pray that we may be strong in our faith to the last.
That we may know Christ
and the power of his resurrection.

We pray for all who have died in faith,
who know Christ and the power of the resurrection,
for all who now share in his victory over the grave,
    especially . . . .
May we live as those who believe and trust
    in the communion of saints,
the forgiveness of sins,
and the resurrection to life everlasting.
That we may know Christ
and the power of his resurrection.

THE PEACE

God the Father give you grace, glory and peace for ever; and the
peace of the Lord be always with you
and also with you.

THE BLESSING

Now to him who is able to keep you from falling,
and to bring you to his everlasting glory,
to our Saviour Jesus Christ,
be praise and glory, dominion and power;
and the blessing...

Proper 23

Sunday between 9 and 15 October inclusive

———

Track 1
Exodus 32. 1–14
Ps. 106. 1–6 [19–23]
Philippians 4. 1–9
Matthew 22. 1–14

Track 2
Isaiah 25. 1–9
Ps. 23
Philippians 4. 1–9
Matthew 22. 1–14

Lord, your mercy reaches to the heavens,
your goodness knows no end.
Let your love and peace be known among us,
that we may draw others to worship you;
through Jesus Christ our Lord. **Amen.**

We give thanks for our faith, and pray for all who struggle in
    the work of the gospel,
for those who preach the word and administer the sacraments.
We pray for a gentleness and graciousness
    in our mission and outreach.
We remember those who work among the outcasts
    and the poor.
We pray for all who strive to bring in your peace.
Lord, by your power and your presence
provide us with peace.

We pray for all troubled areas of your world,
that wars may cease and that we may find a lasting peace.
We pray for the peacemakers of our world.
We remember all who have suffered through war,
all who have been injured,
all who have lost loved ones.
We pray for those whose memories are scarred by violence.
Lord, by your power and your presence
provide us with peace.

We pray that our homes may be places of peace and healing.
We pray for all who are suffering from broken relationships.
We pray for reconciliation and healing where peoples are divided,
that we may live at peace with all people.
Lord, by your power and your presence
provide us with peace.

We pray for all who are distressed,
for the over-anxious and the fearful,
for the troubled in body, mind or spirit,
for all who are over-tense or uptight,
for all who find it hard to relax or let go.
We pray for all whose peace is disturbed
    by the violence or carelessness of others,
that we all may know your presence
    and the peace that you offer.

Lord, by your power and your presence
provide us with peace.

We give thanks for all who have passed through death
and are at peace in your nearer presence.
We pray for friends and loved ones departed from us, especially
for . . . .
May we with them share in the peace of your everlasting
kingdom.
Lord, by your power and your presence
provide us with peace.

THE PEACE

Accept God's peace, think of peace,
speak of peace, act in peace,
pray for peace;
and the peace of the Lord be always with you
and also with you.

THE BLESSING

The peace of the Father be yours,
the peace of the Saviour be yours,
the peace of the Spirit be yours;
and the blessing . . .

Proper 24

Sunday between 16 and 22 October inclusive

———

Track 1
Exodus 33. 12–23
Ps. 99. 1–9 [10–13]
1 Thessalonians 1. 1–10
Matthew 22. 15–22

Track 2
Isaiah 45. 1–7
Ps. 96. 1–9 [10–13]
1 Thessalonians 1. 1–10
Matthew 22. 15–22

God of grace and peace,
we rejoice that you have chosen us,
and empowered us by your Spirit.
Lead us, that we may lead others,
guide us, that we may be the people you would have us be.
Direct us, that we may do what you would have us do;
through Christ the Prince of peace. **Amen.**

May we show your love and your salvation in our lives,
that the church may ever order its priorities,
that it may grow in holiness and in outreach.
We pray for the mission of your church to all who are trapped
    by materialism.
We remember all those fooled by the glitter and false promises
    of our society.
Spirit of God,
guide us and strengthen us.

We pray for all who hunger for goodness and righteousness,
for all who serve you by serving others.
We pray for world leaders and all who influence our future,

for all those who work with the press or broadcasting,
for artists, musicians and writers,
for all who seek to care for and improve our environment.
Spirit of God,
guide us and strengthen us.

May we set a good example by the way we live.
Let our homes be places of grace and goodness,
of hospitality and holiness.
We pray for good relationships and honest dealings.
We remember homes where loved ones are betrayed,
where relationships are breaking down.
Spirit of God,
guide us and strengthen us.

We pray for all who are weak,
for the weak-willed and the weak-minded,
for all who are led into crime or vice.
We pray for all who work for the rehabilitation of addicts or
    criminals.
We pray for those who have lost their way
    and are caught up in darkness.
We remember the depressed, the despairing,
    and all who have lost vision or hope.
We pray for all in sickness, especially for..............
Spirit of God,
guide us and strengthen us.

We entrust to your power our friends and loved ones in this
    world,
and those who have departed from our sight.
We pray that we may all at the last share in the joy and peace of
    your kingdom.
Spirit of God,
guide us and strengthen us.

THE PEACE

The peace of the All-powerful One be with you.
The peace of the Saviour be with you.
The peace of the Strengthener be with you.
The peace of the Lord be always with you
and also with you.

THE BLESSING

The Lord shield you and protect you,
the Lord look upon you and be gracious to you,
the Lord fill you with joy and peace;
and the blessing...

Proper 25

Sunday between 23 and 29 October inclusive

———

Track 1	Track 2
Deuteronomy 34. 1–12	Leviticus 19. 1–2, 15–18
Ps. 90. 1–6 [13–17]	Ps. 1
1 Thessalonians 2. 1–8	1 Thessalonians 2. 1–8
Matthew 22. 34–46	Matthew 22. 34–46

Father, we give you thanks and praise
for all who have had the courage to speak out boldly for the
    gospel,
for all the saints and martyrs of the past,
for holy men and women who now stand for justice and freedom.

May we join with them in serving you;
through Jesus Christ our Lord. **Amen.**

We pray for all who have shared their lives and their faith with
    us.
We pray for all who teach the faith,
for preachers and evangelists,
for theological colleges,
for Religious Education teachers,
for Sunday-school teachers.
We remember all who have been led astray
    by false teachers and vain promises.
Lord of grace and glory,
lead us from despair to hope.

We pray for all who are working for peace in our world,
for all who stand up for the exploited or the underdog,
for those with vision who seek to care for and conserve our
    planet.
We pray for ecologists,
for all who work on the land,
for all research workers and scientists.
We pray for all who have been cheated out of their land by
    economic powers.
Lord of grace and glory,
lead us from despair to hope.

We give thanks for all who share their lives with us and are dear
    to us.
We pray for a spirit of good neighbourliness in our
    communities;
may no one be neglected or forgotten.
We pray for all who are estranged from their loved ones and
    friends.
We pray for the building up of community life,
for community centres and places where locals can meet.

Lord of grace and glory,
lead us from despair to hope.

We remember before you all who are lonely,
all who have been deserted by loved ones,
those who have recently lost a loved one.
We pray for all who have difficulty in making relationships,
for all those in difficult relationships
and where there is a breakdown in understanding or care.
We pray for all who are separated from loved ones through
   sickness,
all who are in hospital or in care.
Lord of grace and glory,
lead us from despair to hope.

We give thanks for all who have sought to love you
   with all their heart, with all their soul and with all their mind.
We remember all who have served you by serving others.
We give thanks for all who in the past have enriched our lives
   and our neighbourhood by their goodness.
We pray that we may have a share with them in your kingdom
   in glory.
Lord of grace and glory,
lead us from despair to hope.
THE PEACE

Delight in the Lord in his love and light
Proclaim his peace by day and by night
The peace of the Lord be always with you
and also with you.

THE BLESSING

The love of God be in your heart,
The peace of God be in your mind,
The grace of God be in your dealings:
and the blessing . . .

Bible Sunday

Neh. 8. 1–4a [5–6], 8–12 : Ps. 119. 9–16 : Colossians 3. 12–17 :
Matthew 24. 30–35

We give you thanks for Scripture writers and translators.
We pray for Bible Societies, Bible study groups, theological
students.
We pray that your church may be true to the Scriptures,
that we may find joy in proclaiming the gospel,
that your word may influence all our actions,
that we may seek to know your word and to obey it,
that we may rejoice in the Word made flesh,
and show that he dwells among us.
Word of life,
reveal to us your glory.

We pray for all who guide and affect the thinking of others,
for leaders of nations and politicians,
for all broadcasters on radio and television,
for those who produce our daily papers.
We pray for writers, actors, musicians, and artists,
for all research workers and inventors.
Word of life,
reveal to us your glory.

We give thanks for those who taught us the good news,
for those who opened the Scriptures to us,
for those who shared their understanding of the Bible,

for all who have brought the word alive
  and introduced us to the Word of Life.
We pray for all who are without knowledge of the Scriptures,
all who are unaware of the living God.
We pray for all whose lives are darkened by fear,
  by lack of faith,
for all who struggle without any knowledge of the love of God,
for all whose lives seem meaningless to them,
for all who are devalued and have no self-esteem.
We remember all who are in sickness or in trouble.
Word of life,
reveal to us your glory.

We give thanks for all who have found guidance and solace
  through the Scriptures,
for all who have come to know Christ as the living Word.
We rejoice with all who have entered the fullness of eternal life.
We pray especially for . . . .
Word of life,
reveal to us your glory.

THE PEACE

Let the word of the Lord be a light to your feet and a guide to
your path; and the peace of the Lord be always with you
and also with you.

THE BLESSING

The Creator of all be about you,
the Word made flesh be within you,
the Spirit ever guide you and sustain you;
and the blessing . . .

Dedication Festival

The First Sunday in October or Last Sunday after Trinity

———

1 Kings 8. 22–30 *or* Revelation 21. 9–14 : Ps. 122 : Hebrews 12. 18–24 :
Matthew 21. 12–16

We give you thanks and praise for this church,
for all who have here found healing and peace,
for all who have found new hope and forgiveness,
for all who have bowed before you in love and worship.
May all who come find this a holy place,
a presence-filled place,
a place of renewal, of refreshment and of service;
through Christ our Lord, who lives and reigns
with the Father and the Holy Spirit in glory for ever. **Amen.**

Lord, as we know a holy place, let us find all places holy.
May we see you at work in your world.
Teach us to treat your creation with awe and respect.
We pray today for builders and planners,
for architects and artists,
for musicians and craftspeople.
Lord of the church,
keep us true to you.

We give thanks for those who brought us into the fellowship of
the church.
We give thanks for the church and its work in our community.
We pray for a respect for one another,

that we may strive for peace, fellowship and healing within our
  society,
that we may be aware of the holiness that is all about us.
Lord of the church,
keep us true to you.

We pray for all unable to come to church
  through sickness, weakness or any disability.
We pray for all who receive house communion,
all visited by church members,
all visited by hospital chaplains,
that we may see the church at work in the healing done in
  hospitals.
Lord of the church,
keep us true to you.

We give thanks for all who have worshipped here
  and are now with the church victorious;
for all who have found peace here
  and are now in the fullness of your peace.
We join with them and with the communion of all your saints,
to praise you now and for ever.
Lord of the church,
keep us true to you.

THE PEACE

The Lord of all directs you to proclaim the good news to the
poor, to go and bind up the broken-hearted.
The peace of the Lord be always with you
and also with you.

THE BLESSING

The Lord, who has called you to serve him, make you worthy of
your calling; and the blessing . . .

All Saints' Day

Sunday between 30 October and 5 November or,
if this is not kept as All Saints' Sunday, on 1 November itself

---

Revelation 7. 9–17 : Ps. 34. 1–10 : 1 John 3. 1–3 : Matthew 5. 1–12

Glory to you, O Lord,
from the whole company of heaven,
from the saints in glory,
from your people on earth.
Father, we give you thanks that in the darkness of this world
    your saints shine.
May we, with them, have a share in your everlasting kingdom;
through Christ our Lord. **Amen.**

We give you praise for holy men and women
    who have been an inspiration to us,
for those who have set us an example to follow.
We remember those who were fully dedicated
    to you and your glory,
those holy martyrs who looked forward to entering your
    kingdom,
men and women who stood up for the faith,
    and set themselves against evil.
May your church be inspired by their lives,
seek to keep before it their dedication,
and follow after their vision.
We pray for all who are seeking to fulfil their vocation,

for all who seek to quietly dedicate themselves
   to you and your glory.
Lord of the saints,
strengthen our faith.

Blessed are you, Lord our God. You have called us to a world
   full of good things.
We thank you for all who have set out to improve our world.
We pray for all who work in conservation,
for those who care for others,
for all who have sacrificed themselves in the service of others,
for those who seek to live simply that others may simply live.
Lord of the saints,
strengthen our faith.

We give you thanks for those who taught us the faith,
for those who gave generously and sacrificially for us,
for all who have led us in the ways of goodness and truth.
We pray that our homes and our work may be places of
   holiness,
that we may be an example to others.
Lord of the saints,
strengthen our faith.

We pray for all who are being persecuted or suffering for their
   faith,
all who are facing mockery and scorn,
all whose faith is being tested at this time.
We pray for all in sickness
and for those approaching death.
Lord of the saints,
strengthen our faith.

Lord, grant us a share in the inheritance of your saints in glory.
May we at the last be part of the church which is victorious.
We give thanks today for all your saints,
   especially . . . .

and we join our praises with theirs.
Lord of the saints,
strengthen our faith.

THE PEACE

Be strong through the grace that is yours in union with Christ
Jesus; and the peace of the Lord be always with you
and also with you.

THE BLESSING

Be of good courage, stand firm in the faith, do everything in
love; and the blessing...

Sundays Before Advent

The Fourth Sunday Before Advent

Sunday between 30 October and 5 November inclusive.
For use if the Feast of All Saints was celebrated on 1 November
and alternative propers are needed.

———

Micah 3. 5–12 : Ps. 43 (*or* Ps. 107. 1–8) : 1 Thessalonians 2. 9–13 :
Matthew 24. 1–14

Holy God, Holy and Strong One, Holy and Mighty One,
we rejoice in your presence,
we live by your power.
Keep us in your peace;
through Christ, the living Lord. **Amen.**

We give you thanks for all who have encouraged and
    strengthened us in the faith,
for our early teachers, for preachers,
for faithful witnesses.
We pray to you for the world-wide church,
that it may lead people to your love, your peace, your joy;
above all that it may draw many to know your presence and
    your grace.
We pray for those who suffer for their faith, and get little
    support.
Lord, inspire us
and fill us with your grace.

We pray for all who are burdened by heavy loads,
for countries and individuals who are deeply in debt,
for all who live among chaos and confusion,
for all who suffer from earthquakes or famine,
for all who are subjected to wars and rumours of wars,
for displaced persons and refugees.
Lord, inspire us
and fill us with your grace.

We give you thanks for our homes and for all who have been a
good support.
We remember before you our loved ones and our close friends.
We pray for a sense of joy and liberty in the communities to
which we belong,
that we may be forgiving and understanding in our dealings.
Lord, inspire us
and fill us with your grace.

We pray for all who find life severe,
all who are hard on themselves and on others.
We pray for all with deep burdens of guilt.
Lord, be a strength to the weak,
bring hope to the fearful, and peace to the troubled.
Ease the heavy-burdened,
be a guide to all who have erred and strayed.
We pray for the sick, and especially for . . . .
Lord, inspire us
and fill us with your grace.

We rejoice in your love and forgiveness.
We pray that the departed may know your mercy and grace.
May we all come to know your loving acceptance in your
glorious kingdom.
Lord, inspire us
and fill us with your grace.

THE PEACE

Trust in the Lord, the eternal Rock, that he may keep your
mind in perfect peace; and the peace of the Lord be always with
you
and also with you.

THE BLESSING

The Lord look upon you and refresh you,
the Lord, in his mercy, restore you,
the Lord, in his love, strengthen you;
and the blessing . . .

The Third Sunday Before Advent

Sunday between 6 and 12 November inclusive

———

Wisdom of Solomon 6. 12–16 & *Canticle:* Wisdom of Solomon 6. 17–20 :
or Amos 5. 18–24 & Ps. 70 : 1 Thessalonians 4. 13–18 : Matthew 25. 1–13

Lord awaken us to your glory.
Open our eyes to your presence,
open our ears to your call,
open our hearts to your love,
that we may give ourselves to you,
and work to your praise and glory. **Amen.**

Lord, let us be ever vigilant in our watching for you.
You come to us, make us aware of you.
Bless your church, that it may know you and love you,
that it may love you and serve you,
that it may serve you and proclaim you,
that it may proclaim you and enjoy you for ever.
Lord, your kingdom come,
your will be done.

Come, Lord, to your people who yearn for your peace.
Come to your people who cry for your love.
Come to your people who search for your joy.
Come to all who walk in darkness, and bring your light.
We pray that the kingdoms of the world may become
    the kingdom of Christ our Lord.
Lord, your kingdom come,
your will be done.

Come to our homes and reveal your love.
Come, heal our divisions.
Increase our faith in you and in each other.
Strengthen our fellowship through your presence.
Guide our actions by the power of your Spirit.
We pray for our friends, and for all that we share.
Lord, your kingdom come,
your will be done.

We remember before you all who are world-weary.
We pray for those who are weary of serving others,
for those who are weary of their own lives,
for lives that lack love, joy or peace,
for all who have lost hope.
We pray for healers and for peacemakers.
We remember all who are in sickness.
Lord, your kingdom come,
your will be done.

We give thanks for all who have triumphed over darkness and
  death,
for the great kingdom of the redeemed.
We entrust to you our homes, our friends and loved ones,
and pray that we may share with your saints in everlasting
  glory.
Lord, your kingdom come,
your will be done.

THE PEACE

The Lord is your defence and shield; a very present help in
  trouble.
The peace of the Lord be always with you
and also with you.

THE BLESSING

The Lord keep you close to his heart,
the Lord gather you into his arms,
the Lord lead you into paths of peace;
and the blessing...

The Second Sunday Before Advent

Sunday between 13 and 19 November inclusive

Zephaniah 1. 7, 12–18 : Ps. 90. 1–8 [9–12] : 1 Thessalonians 5. 1–11 :
Matthew 25. 14–30

Lord, we pray that we may be found ready at your coming:
may we heed your call and do your will.
Guide your church that it may show forth your light and love;
through Christ our Lord. **Amen.**

Bless the mission of the church, as it seeks to reveal your
    kingdom.
May we be seen as children of the day, and not of the night,
that we may encourage and build up one another in the faith,
that each of us may use our talents to the benefit of others and
    to your glory.
We pray for all evangelists and preachers of the word.
Saviour of the world,
save us and help us.

We remember before you all those who exercise their gifts in
    government, in commerce, in the building up of society.
We pray for those whose talents cannot be used
    through no fault of their own:
the world poor, the oppressed, the troubled.
We remember all who are frustrated in their work
    or in their lives.
We pray for those whose world is collapsing around them.

Saviour of the world,
save us and help us.

We rejoice in the gifts you have given to us;
may we share them and use them aright.
We pray for specially talented people,
for musicians and artists,
for writers and craftspeople,
for scientists and research workers,
for creators and inventors.
Saviour of the world,
save us and help us.

We remember all who are handicapped,
all who cannot enter into the fullness of life.
We pray for those with limited mobility,
for those who cannot communicate clearly,
for all with impaired vision or hearing.
We pray for the autistic,
for all who have suffered damage to their limbs or brain.
We remember all in sickness, and pray especially
    for...............
Saviour of the world,
save us and help us.

We rejoice in the saints of God,
all who have triumphed over their disabilities
  and now have the glorious liberty of the children of God.
We pray for friends and loved ones departed,
    especially..............
Saviour of the world,
save us and help us.

Grace and peace to you, from him who is, and who was, and who is to come; and the peace of the Lord be always with you **and also with you.**

THE BLESSING

Be strong in the Lord and in the power of his might; let the word of God dwell in you; and the blessing...

Christ the King

Sunday between 20 and 26 November inclusive

Ezekiel 34. 11–16, 20–24 : Ps. 95. 1–7a [7b] : Ephesians 1. 15–23 :
Matthew 25. 31–46

You are the king of glory, O Christ,
you are the everlasting Son of the Father.
May your kingdom come in us on earth,
as it is in heaven, Christ our Lord. **Amen.**

Christ, we confess you as King of kings and Lord of lords;
come, rule in our hearts and claim us as part of your kingdom.
We seek to dedicate our lives to you and to your glory.
We pray for all who are working for the bringing in of your
    kingdom,
for those striving for justice, peace and freedom,
for all relief agencies and bringers of aid.

Lord, we seek to do your will.
Your kingdom come in us as it is in heaven.

We pray for rulers of peoples, for leaders of nations,
that they may govern with gentleness and integrity.
We remember all who suffer from injustice.
We pray for the scorned and rejected people of our world,
for all who have lost their freedom,
for all who are deprived of their basic rights.
We pray for the work of Amnesty International.
Lord, we seek to do your will.
Your kingdom come in us as it is in heaven.

Come, Lord, rule in our hearts.
Come, Lord, rule in our homes.
Come, Lord, rule in our lives.
Come, Lord, and transform your people.
Lord, we seek to do your will.
Your kingdom come in us as it is in heaven.

We pray for all who are struggling,
for all who cannot cope.
We remember weak people needing protection,
lost people longing for salvation.
We remember the hungry, thirsty, and naked,
the prisoners and the homeless.
We pray for friends and loved ones who are in need.
Lord, we seek to do your will.
Your kingdom come in us as it is in heaven.

Christ, O King, ruler of heaven and earth,
in you we triumph over darkness and death,
in you we have life eternal.
We pray for all our loved ones departed this life,
that they may be one with you and your saints
    in your everlasting kingdom;
and that we, setting our hearts on things above,

may be raised up to where you reign
   with the Father and the Holy Spirit for ever.
Lord, we seek to do your will.
Your kingdom come in us as it is in heaven.

THE PEACE

God, who called you to his eternal glory in Christ, make you
strong to do his will; and the peace of the Lord be always with
you
and also with you.

THE BLESSING

To him who is able to keep you from falling,
to Christ our King and our Saviour,
be praise and glory, majesty and power
for ever and ever;
and the blessing...